S0-FJM-565

FACSIMILES OF
ORIGINAL CHARTERS AND WRITS
OF KING STEPHEN
THE EMPRESS MATILDA AND
DUKES GEOFFREY AND HENRY
1135–1154

REGESTA REGUM
ANGLO-NORMANNORUM
1066–1154

VOLUME IV

FACSIMILES OF
ORIGINAL CHARTERS AND WRITS
OF KING STEPHEN
THE EMPRESS MATILDA AND
DUKES GEOFFREY AND HENRY
1135–1154

EDITED BY

H. A. CRONNE

AND

R. H. C. DAVIS

IN CONTINUATION OF THE WORK OF
THE LATE

H. W. C. DAVIS

OXFORD
AT THE CLARENDON PRESS
MDCCCCLXIX

Oxford University Press, Ely House, London W. 1

GLASGOW NEW YORK TORONTO MELBOURNE WELLINGTON
CAPE TOWN SALISBURY IBADAN NAIROBI LUSAKA ADDIS ABABA
BOMBAY CALCUTTA MADRAS KARACHI LAHORE DACCA
KUALA LUMPUR HONG KONG SINGAPORE TOKYO

942.01
& R262
v 4

184996

© OXFORD UNIVERSITY PRESS 1969

PRINTED IN GREAT BRITAIN
AT THE UNIVERSITY PRESS, OXFORD
BY VIVIAN RIDLER
PRINTER TO THE UNIVERSITY

LAUS DEO

PREFACE

THE publication of this, the concluding, volume of *Regesta Regum Anglo-Normannorum* has been made possible by a generous grant from the British Academy, which it gives us great pleasure to acknowledge. The work itself could not have been attempted but for recent important contributions to scholarship in this field, especially those of Mr. T. A. M. Bishop and Dr. P. Chaplais, both individually and in collaboration. We have made constant use of Mr. Bishop's *Scriptores Regis*, accepting his identification and adopting his enumeration of the scribes who served Henry I, Stephen, the Empress, and Duke Henry. His work has made possible a study of the style and draftsmanship of individual royal scribes, opening up thereby a new dimension in the diplomatic of Anglo-Norman royal charters and writs which we have attempted to explore. From Dr. Chaplais we have learned much about sigillography as well as diplomatic. Besides our debt to the published works of Mr. Bishop and Dr. Chaplais, we gratefully acknowledge how much we owe to their personal kindness; to the material, the information, the advice, and the help so generously given by them. Our greatest debts are to Professor V. H. Galbraith for his inspiration, encouragement, admonition, instruction, and example during many years (and to him our collaboration is due); to the late Charles Johnson and especially to the founder and first editor of this work, the late H. W. C. Davis. It has been a privilege as well as a responsibility to try to follow in the footsteps of such predecessors. We wish also to record our thanks to Professor G. W. S. Barrow and Professor C. R. Cheney for much assistance and valuable advice. We would also express our gratitude to the owners and custodians of muniments and archives who have given us permission to reproduce documents: to the Trustees of the British Museum, the Keeper of the Public Records, the Bodleian Library and Dr. Richard Hunt, Keeper of the Western Manuscripts, the Directeur Généraldes Archives de France, the Countess of Sutherland, the Duke of Rutland, the Marquess of Anglesey, the Deans and Chapters of Ely, Exeter, Gloucester, London, Salisbury, and Westminster, the Provost and Fellows of King's College, Cambridge, Keele University, the William Salt Library, Stafford, the Gloucestershire Records Office, the Shropshire Record Office, Beverley Corporation, and to E. Willes Esq.; to Mr. A. R. B. Fuller, Archivist of St. Paul's, Mrs. R. A. Erskine of Exeter Cathedral Library, Mr. I. Gray, Gloucester County Archivist, Dr. L. E. Tanner, and Mr. N. H. MacMichael, Keeper of the Muniments and Library, Westminster Abbey, and Mrs. D. M. Owen, Ely Diocesan Archivist. We are especially indebted to Sir Charles Clay for information about a hitherto unrecorded charter of Stephen at Loxley Hall, Warwick, to Colonel A. Gregory-Hood for permission to reproduce it, and both to him and to Dr. Levi Fox, Director of the Shakespeare Birthplace Trust, for the trouble they took to have this charter photographed. We feel a deep sense of obligation to the archivists of every record office and repository, where relevant charters are preserved, for their helpfulness and patience. We are, lastly, but not least, indebted to the staff of the Delegates of the Oxford University Press, without whose technical advice and help this volume of facsimiles could not have been produced.

In compiling the volume we have worked upon the principle that every original Anglo-Norman royal charter and writ is worth reproducing in facsimile, since only by comparing documents in widely scattered collections can we determine which are forgeries and which are genuine. Although no reproduction, whether in collotype or, as in this volume, by a fine-screen offset process, can take the place of an original manuscript, it enables features to be observed which cannot always be accurately indicated in a printed text. It may also preserve a record of documents which disappear or become damaged as, unfortunately, they still do. We have tried to give a representative selection, mainly from those which have not previously been published in facsimile, of original royal charters and writs of the period 1135–54. Approximately one half of all the surviving originals of this period will now be available in facsimile in this volume and scattered in other publications. A complete list is included in this volume together with their locations. We have included a number of forgeries for comparison with the genuine examples and also the genuine and forged First Seals and the Second Seal of King Stephen and the Seal of the Empress. Save for the three surviving exemplifications of the 'Oxford Charter of Liberties' of 1136, which have been brought together, and two Norman Charters of Dukes Geoffrey and Henry, the documents are arranged according to their scribes and, within this arrangement, chronologically as far as possible, so that the degree of uniformity achieved by each scribe, both in external appearance and in the drafting of his documents, may be observed. In each case we have given the source of the document and the number of its text in *Regesta*, vol. iii, which, since we have tried to avoid needless repetition, we have assumed will be used side by side with this volume. We also give the date-limits to which we assign each document and a brief abstract of its contents together with notes on its diplomatic structure and other points of interest.

Just as the previous volume was primarily the work of Davis, so the present volume is primarily the work of Cronne.

H. A. C.
R. H. C. D.

1967

INTRODUCTION

THE purpose of diplomatic is to elucidate the form which any given documentary instrument takes in a given place at a given time. In the case of English royal charters and writs of the first half of the twelfth century, a very large proportion of which have a direct legal significance, their diplomatic construction must have been determined by the formulas, still in process of evolution, which were necessary to meet the legal requirements of the law courts. In our view, the nature of English royal diplomata from the earliest times must have been determined by the formalized procedure of Anglo-Saxon courts and by the verbal and symbolic rituals which accompanied grants of landed and other property, privileges, franchises, and exemptions, and the putting of grantees in possession of these. The symbolic public ceremony was, for long, all that was formally necessary for the transfer of property and rights. When written records of such transactions came to be made they were, at first, in the nature of precautionary evidences rather than, strictly, instruments of conveyance. They must, however, have followed closely the wording of the traditional oral procedure, alliterative in form and mnemonic in intention, because of the legal implications which it bore. When writs came to be used increasingly for legal as well as administrative purposes it was, presumably, necessary to employ in them formulas determined by the usages and requirements of the law courts. So, it seems likely, traditional phrases acquired a documentary form and passed into Anglo-Norman usage, often retaining the old wording when this had lost much, if not all, of its former significance. A society which evolved and maintained the process of *miskenning* because, fundamentally, so many of those concerned in litigation must have been illiterate, was highly formalistic in its legal practice and was likely still to insist upon the letter of the traditional formulas when it advanced to the stage of using the written word. Indeed they remained to a great extent in their Old English form in the Latin charters and writs of the Norman kings. *Miskenning*, however, was an anachronism by the twelfth century and most boroughs, for example, which contrived, like London (1130), to obtain early charters of liberties, got rid of this frustrating and expensive procedure in their courts and in cases in which their burgesses were involved. This is a straw in the wind of change and we may expect to find, as indeed we do, that the traditional mnemonic formulas are in process of being reduced to a minimal form in twelfth-century charters and writs and that new kinds of legal clauses are gradually being evolved.

The rapid development of law in England after the Norman Conquest, especially under the aegis of Henry I and under the influence of the upsurging interest in legal studies, which characterized the twelfth century, is a commonplace of history. In fact the precise nature of this development in English law is still obscure in many of its details. There tends to be too much unwarranted reading back into the first half of the twelfth century, and earlier, of the legal practices of the later years of Henry II; too strong a tendency to try to relate earlier procedure directly to what we find in Glanvill. There are still too many missing links and the temptation to manufacture them is understandably difficult to resist. The author of *Leges Henrici Primi*, himself probably a royal justice, bears explicit witness to the bewildering rapidity of legal change, which baffled many contemporaries:

> Law varies through the shires as the avarice and sinister, odious activity of legal experts add more grievous means of injury to established legal process. There is so much perversity and such affluence of evil that the certain truth of law and the remedy established by settled provision can rarely be found, but to the great confusion of all a new method of pleading is sought out, a new subtlety of injury found. . . . Legal process is involved in so many and so great anxieties and deceits that men avoid these actions and the uncertain dice of pleas.[1]

Law was clearly increasing in complexity as new processes were developed. It is often difficult to discern from royal writs exactly what effect the crown's intervention in litigation had; it sometimes seems almost irresponsible. The author of the *Leges* thought that law was being exploited as a source of profit ('it is the desire for wealth that brings this madness upon us') and there is no room for doubt about the steady determination of the Norman kings to draw their profits from justice and to extend the effective scope of royal jurisdiction. The brazen, mercenary intervention of the crown in the administration of justice can be seen on almost every membrane of Henry I's surviving Pipe Roll. The Norman settlement in England with all its dynastic, family, and feudal complications, the activities of royal ministers, especially such as Flambard and Henry I's 'new men', and the fact that the Normans were an exceedingly litigious people, gave endless cause for litigation and for profitable royal intervention.

The remarkably large number of writs emerging from the royal Scriptorium in the reigns of Henry I and Stephen, as compared with those of William I and William II, bears striking witness to the growth of administration by the written word, to the extent and complexity of litigation and legal processes, and to the spreading influence of royal justice, even in spite of all the difficulties of Stephen's disturbed reign. It is clear that many churches, groups of laymen such as burgesses and gilds, and individuals both clerical and lay went to much trouble and expense to obtain charters and writs from Stephen. Even forgers did not disdain to fabricate them. We may reasonably conclude that, even if they were not always effectual, they were considered of value and importance in establishing rights in property, possession, and privileges. Unfortunately the precise function of some of these writs and the stages in litigation that they may represent are not fully understood by legal historians. In an age of changing legal processes and the slow, often hesitant, replacement of archaic by newer methods, we cannot expect a strict uniformity in the documents involved. The scribes who drafted them may themselves have been a little uncertain at times about their correct formulation. Administrative expertise was not yet sufficiently advanced fully to grasp the important principle of using a single, uniform type of document for a specific purpose and the no less important principle of avoiding multi-purpose documents, which are very likely to lead to confusion. In Glanvill we can see that such principles were beginning to be grasped. It is only by a comparative study of the royal writs of the first half of the twelfth century and earlier with those of the Glanvill era that we can fully appreciate the calibre of the legal and administrative genius that made possible the great reforms of Henry II's reign.

Professor van Caenegem has made a most notable and scholarly contribution in

---

[1] *Leges Henrici Primi*, 6. 3a–6. 6, ed. F. Liebermann in *Die Gesetze der Angelsachsen*. Translation from F. M. Stenton, *The First Century of English Feudalism* (1961), 220.

this field of study,[1] but we confess to some hesitation in accepting his assignment of earlier writs to the legal categories found in Glanvill, especially as a not inconsiderable number of these 'emergent prototypes' of the later writs have to be assigned to two or more categories at the same time. Certain matters, however, such as *seisin*, *ius* and *hereditas*, *defectus iusticie* and *penuria recti*, must have been of increasing concern and importance because we see them with growing frequency in royal writs. With these matters courts of all kinds and especially the royal justices must have been more and more concerned: indeed the increasing frequency with which justices and sheriffs are addressed in association is significant. The formulas which these legal matters required were naturally tending towards the stereotyping which is so highly developed in Glanvill, but this had not yet been fully achieved in the middle of the century. It is possible to say that a specific writ of Stephen, **536** for example, looks like an evolving writ of *Mort d'Ancestor*. Again **552** may look like a writ *De Nativo Habendo*, though it seems to us to be, rather, a writ for execution of judgment following a successful claim by Henry Bishop of Winchester, for the recovery of his *nativus*, Mud by name. What we cannot assert about these and other categories of royal writs of Henry I and Stephen is that they are standardized like the later 'writs of course'. In consequence of this, the diplomatic study of the writs of the Norman kings, especially Henry I and Stephen, is bound to present difficulties and sure diplomatic criteria of authenticity for these writs must remain elusive.

Our own investigations have added materially to the uncertainties of the situation because they have raised certain doubts about widely accepted criteria of authenticity of charters and writs.[2] It may be said at once and unequivocally that the only sure guarantee (if sure it be) of the authenticity of a charter or writ of the period with which we are concerned is now, as it was then, the attachment to it of a genuine seal which, as far as can be discerned, has not been tampered with. But how far, after the lapse of so many centuries and the almost inevitable damaging of the seals, can traces of skilful manipulation be discerned or, indeed, how reliable are the criteria by which we judge the authenticity of seals? It is not very long since Dr. Chaplais demonstrated the existence of forged seals of Henry I far more numerous than had hitherto been suspected.[3] The seal-forger was no *rara avis* in the twelfth century. There is, for example, an interesting account of how Ralph Abbot of St. Albans (1146–51) dismissed his prior, Alquin, because he strongly suspected him of attempting to procure a forgery of the abbatial seal. A monk named Ansketil, a goldsmith of the King of Denmark, was staying in the abbey at the time and a seal-matrix, not yet engraved, was found on his workbench.[4]

We, like twelfth-century authorities, must look to our seals with the utmost care. Broadly speaking, we are obliged to accept as genuine an ostensible royal seal of which we have a number of clearly identifiable examples, which have not been tampered with and which are properly appended to documents with no suspicious

---

[1] R. C. van Caenegem, *Royal Writs in England from the Conquest to Glanvill* (Selden Soc. 77, 1959).

[2] For these criteria see T. A. M. Bishop and P. Chaplais, *Facsimiles of English Royal Writs to A.D. 1100 Presented to Vivian Hunter Galbraith* (Oxford, The Clarendon Press, 1957), xv ff. and T. A. M. Bishop, *Scriptores Regis* (Oxford, The Clarendon Press, 1961), 15 ff.

[3] P. Chaplais, 'Seals and original charters of Henry I', in *E.H.R.* lxxxvi (1960), 260–75. See also Bishop and Chaplais, op. cit., and T. F. T. Plucknett, 'Deeds and Seals', in *T.R.H.S.*, 4th ser. xxxii (1950), 150–1, where the legal significance of the seal is emphasized.

[4] *Gesta Abbatum Mon. S. Albani a Thoma Walsingham*, ed. T. H. Riley (R.S. 1867), i. 107.

features, issued on different occasions for different beneficiaries. It is all the better if these documents are written in the hands of identifiable royal scribes (for whom the criteria are very similar). Such seals must pass the kind of critical scrutiny which Innocent III recommended to the Archdeacon of Milan for dealing with suspect papal bulls.[1] The closest attention was to be paid to every smallest detail of the *bulla* itself, down to the merest dots. But the pope pointed out that even a genuine leaden *bulla*, on its hempen or silken cords, might be manipulated in a number of ways so that it might be detached and appended to a forged document well enough to pass a casual and uncritical inspection. It might be prised open far enough at the edges for the strings to be cut below the surface, or even completely withdrawn, so as to be re-threaded through a forged document and reinserted in the *bulla*, the edges of which could be nipped together again to grip them. A skilful manipulator might even venture upon inconspicuous splicing of strings. Waxen seals upon tongues of parchment perhaps presented a slightly more delicate, but by no means insuperable, problem for the manipulator. Much might be achieved by the skilful use of a heated needle or knife (an operation in which women were thought to excel) to enable a genuine seal to be split and the two halves fused together again upon a forged document.

We cannot, for example, help entertaining suspicions about a fine impression of Stephen's Second Seal (believed genuine) on a grant of two fairs and a market to Great Bricett Priory.[2] This seal is uncommonly thin and, although obvious signs of tampering have not been detected, it is not impossible that it may have been transferred from another document to which it was originally appended. There are, in fact, other reasons for suspecting the document, even though the nature of the grant and the fact that it was not written by a known royal scribe would not call for adverse comment. It was a common practice for charters written by beneficiaries' scribes to be authenticated by the royal seal, even though their diplomatic construction sometimes differed considerably from the usage of the royal Scriptorium. Our suspicions are aroused because the hand in which the charter is written seems to us a late form for the date to which it should belong if it were genuine, namely, 1153–4. These suspicions are strengthened by the superscription, for it scarcely seems possible that anyone at this date should have given Stephen the title *Dux Normannorum*. Everyone must have known perfectly well by this time that Stephen was not, in fact, Duke of Normandy and that the title now belonged to Henry Plantagenet. In any case, the title *Dux Normannorum* was seldom used in Stephen's genuine charters, even those issued when he was in the Duchy in 1137; nor, indeed, did Henry I commonly use it. There was, however, this excuse for the scribe of the Great Bricett charter, that the title appeared on the equestrian side of Stephen's Second, as of his First, Seal.[3] This might, in fact, support the view that the charter is a forgery, since the scribe may simply have copied the superscription from the legends on the Second Seal, which is appended. In spite, however, of our suspicions, we cannot condemn this Great Bricett charter as definitely false, since it bears a genuine seal which we cannot demonstrate to have been tampered with. The anachronisms may be due simply to the employment by Great Bricett Priory of a scribe who was, as we say nowadays, 'not with it'.

Modern photographic techniques have done much to facilitate the detailed comparative study of seals. An examination of Plates I and II will show how the forger's

---

[1] Baluze, *Epistolae Innocentii III*, 201.   [2] **118**.   [3] See Plate II.

mistakes may be detected, even in quite a small fragment of a seal. This is particularly important in connexion with another point, which we will now consider.

In dealing with original royal charters and writs (we mean here 'original' writs in the archival, not in the legal, sense) it has generally been accepted that, if a number of such be found in the same identifiable handwriting, issued on different occasions for different beneficiaries, they may be regarded as the products of a royal scribe. Further, it has been customary to say that all such originals and any newly discovered examples in the same handwriting may, with a considerable degree of confidence, be accepted as genuine. We have found that, as a working rule, this is not wholly reliable, because circumstances sometimes turned 'gamekeepers into poachers'. In this respect the conditions during Stephen's reign may have been exceptional, but there is ample evidence of the defalcations of royal scribes and clerks in other reigns.[1] Coke mentions a particularly ingenious method by which a royal clerk, George Leak, contrived to get the Great Seal attached to a blank parchment in what was ostensibly the course of his routine work.[2] Coke, however, was concerned only with the main legal issue involved, that is, whether the miscreant was guilty of the crime of Misprision of Treason, so he did not explain the nature of the forgery (if any) that was perpetrated on this sealed parchment, or how the fraud was discovered. We ourselves have found the handwriting of a peculiarly prolific and idiosyncratic royal scribe, Mr. Bishop's Scriptor XIII, in a charter for Reading Abbey which bears on a tongue a fragment of what, we have no doubt, is the forged First Seal of Stephen.[3] Likewise Scriptor XVIII wrote a charter for Worcester Cathedral,[4] which seems to have borne an impression of the same forged seal (now detached). The text of this charter has been tampered with and it is possible that Scriptor XVIII may not have been directly concerned with the use of this forged seal. The same forged seal, or fragments of it, have been discovered on charters for Oseney Abbey (**626**), Rochester Cathedral (**718**), and another for Worcester Cathedral (**964**), all in the hands of unidentified scribes. This looks like a forgery 'ring' which, incredible though it may sound, was not without contemporary parallel.[5]

It is perhaps worth recalling briefly the ramifications of some of these 'rings'. It is well known that the early charters of Westminster Abbey must be treated with profound suspicion and tested with the utmost rigour. The number of blatant forgeries and dubious texts among these muniments is uncommonly large. There is evidence to suggest that, in the middle of the twelfth century, someone at Westminster Abbey was providing other houses, namely, Battle, Coventry, Gloucester, and Ramsey, with fabricated charters and that king Stephen's illegitimate son, abbot Gervase, who was deprived in 1157, may have been concerned in the business and perhaps also the Prior, Osbert of Clare.

The evidence we have found concerning the Oseney–Reading–Rochester–Worcester group bears only upon their common use of the same forged seal. There is nothing to prove that a single individual was responsible for these fabrications; on the contrary,

[1] See L. C. Hector, *Palaeography and Forgery* (St. Anthony's Hall Publications, No. 15, London, 1959).
[2] *Coke's Reports*, Hil. 4 Jac.   [3] **679** and Plate X. Cf. Plates I and II.   [4] **963** and Plate XXIII.
[5] See Wilhelm Levison, *England and the Continent in the Eighth Century* (1946), App. i; Miss F. E. Harmer, *Anglo-Saxon Writs*, 54, 217, 248 ff. and her 'Anglo-Saxon charters and the historian' in *Bulletin of J. Rylands Library*, xii. 339 ff.; Miss J. C. Lancaster in *Bulletin of the Inst. of Hist. Research*, xxvii. 124 ff.; B. W. Scholz, 'Two forged charters from the Abbey of Westminster and their relationship with Saint Denis' in *E.H.R.* lxxv (1961); P. Chaplais in *Pipe Roll Soc.* N.S. xxxvi (1960), 97.

one and possibly two royal scribes are involved together with monastic scribes. Vaguely in the background are Robert de Sigillo Bishop of London, once *Magister Scriptorii* in the service of Henry I and afterwards a monk at Reading, and another Reading monk, the deprived abbot, Reginald, who was said to have served Stephen as deputy-Chancellor. They are not definitely implicated: but there were experts in the Reading cloister and the scribe of the Reading forgery, royal Scriptor XIII, is known to have done some scribal work for Robert de Sigillo Bishop of London.[1] We also regard with some suspicion the Salisbury scribe, three of whose charters are illustrated in Plates XLVIII, XLIX, and L. He may have been the secretary of bishop Roger and he was obviously well acquainted with the formulas and style of the royal Scriptorium. The justiciarial writ (Plate L) may be accepted as perfectly genuine; the charter illustrated in Plate XLVIII is probably genuine, but that shown in Plate XLIX seems to be a distinct 'improvement' upon what was originally intended. This scribe, in fact, poses problems similar to those raised by Scriptor XIII. The manipulation of charters would not have been difficult in a see where the bishop was the great Roger of Salisbury and after his death the bishop-designate was the King's chancellor, Philip de Harcourt.

St. Martin's le Grand, London, may (as we suggested in *Regesta* iii) have enjoyed a similar advantage. We think it possible that Scriptor XIV, whom Mr. Bishop identified as Peter the Scribe, may have been a resident canon or a scribal employee there c. 1145–7. We cannot, however, be absolutely certain that, if indeed Scriptor XIV and not an imitator, as Mr. Bishop suggested,[2] wrote a number of charters for St. Martin's,[3] they were all authentic royal charters. So many charters in the same hand for the same beneficiary inevitably give rise to suspicion (and they are in the hand, or one astonishingly closely resembling that, of a scribe who left the service of Stephen for that of the Empress). On the other hand, it is very difficult to conceive why a scribe legitimately employed by the beneficiaries, or even a forger working for them, should have troubled to imitate, with sustained and quite remarkable success, the hand of one particular royal scribe. It would have been quite a difficult feat and, in twelfth-century conditions and according to twelfth-century notions, utterly unnecessary. Charters written by beneficiaries' scribes seem to have been commonly accepted and authenticated by the royal seal, without the slightest attempt at an 'official' hand. Forgers do not seem to have made a practice of imitating either contemporary 'official' hands or those of an earlier age.[4] In fact, for such an extensive series of forgeries as this group of St. Martin's charters would involve if they were false, a forged seal would probably have been very much more valuable than an imitative hand, which counted for nothing. As we have pointed out, the only seal they muster between them is a genuine one. If we are right in our belief that the hand employed in this series of St. Martin's documents is that of Scriptor XIV himself, a question arises about the capacity in which he wrote them. Had he returned to the royal Scriptorium after his period of employment by the Empress, which seems to have ended not later than early 1144? This seems, on the face of it, unlikely. Apart from other considerations, if he was employed in the service of Stephen again it is peculiar that only his St. Martin's originals have survived from this time. It is possible

---

[1] See Plate XI.   [2] *Scriptores Regis*, 8.   [3] **540, 545, 547, 549, 552, 558.**
[4] This point is well illustrated by Mr. L. C. Hector, in *Palaeography and Forgery*.

that the period between his leaving the service of the Empress and 1147 or 1148, when he entered that of Archbishop Theobald,[1] was occupied in the employment of St. Martin's or as a resident canon there.

Some of these St. Martin's documents were legal and administrative writs of a fairly advanced kind[2] which one would not expect normally to be written by a beneficiary's scribe. They are different from run-of-the-mill grants of land, liberties, quittances, and the like, which were quite often written by beneficiaries' scribes. In the case of one who was a former scriptor regis, even though a turncoat, a greater degree of latitude may have been allowed. It must be remembered, too, that the St. Martin's collection is unusually large and includes writs, representing stages in prolonged litigation, which only the most careful preservers of muniments might have considered worth keeping once the case was settled. If we are confronted in this series of St. Martin's writs with the work of a forger, he was remarkably clever and audacious. Our conclusion is that these writs are in the handwriting of Peter the Scribe himself and that they are genuine (if only because we cannot demonstrate that they are false).

Skilled resident practitioners were no doubt ideal for purposes of forgery, but the services of outside operators seem to have been easily available. So William Cumin, chancellor of David, King of Scots, in his attempt to obtain the see of Durham in 1141, was able to employ a foot-loose Cistercian to fabricate papal bulls in support of his usurpation of the episcopal power and property. What we have called 'rings' of forgery undoubtedly existed in England in this forgers' heyday and international ramifications have been discovered. In the twelfth century there was a prolonged dispute between St. Augustine's Abbey, Canterbury, and the Archbishop concerning the Abbots' professions of canonical obedience. The Abbey claimed exemption on the ground of ancient privileges, which were duly produced for examination. It is sufficient to refer to Gervase's account of the judgment upon these two documents.[3] One, which was alleged to be a privilege of King Ethelbert, was thought to be old, but it had been scraped and there was writing underneath (*rasa et subscripta*) and it was not authenticated by a seal.[4] The other document, said to be a privilege of St. Augustine, no less, was adjudged to merit condemnation because both the writing and the appended *bulla*, with the image of the bishop, were palpably new. It was also said that Cisalpine bishops did not normally use leaden *bullae* and that the form and style of the Latin text did not conform with Roman usage.

This Canterbury episode is one part of a story of forgery. Another has been told by Professor Levison.[5] At the Council of Rheims in October 1131, in the presence of Pope Innocent II, there was a controversy between the newly elected Abbots of Saint Ouen and Jumièges, on the one side, and the Archbishop of Rouen, on the other, about their professions of obedience; the very same thing that disturbed relations between St. Augustine's and the Archbishops of Canterbury. The pope asked whether the two abbots could sustain their claims by authentic privileges. While the

---

[1] *Regesta* iii, xiv.   [2] See, e.g., **545** and **547**.   [3] *Gervase of Canterbury* (R.S.), i. 296.
[4] A seal on such a document would be, for modern scholars, a sure sign of forgery. Anglo-Saxon royal diplomata were not sealed, though writs, when these came into use, were. This fact was not appreciated in early post-Conquest times and led forgers astray; those of Westminster Abbey, for example, who produced several diplomata alleged to have been granted by the Confessor and bearing his seal. See Harmer, op. cit.
[5] See p. 5, *n.* 5.

Abbot of Saint Ouen hesitated to answer, Geoffrey, Bishop of Chalons, made a startling intervention. He explained that when he was abbot of Saint Medard (Soissons) one of his monks, called Guerno, making his deathbed confession, admitted that he was a forger. He said he had provided various churches, including the monasteries of Saint Ouen and St. Augustine's, Canterbury, with forged papal privileges. Saint Medard is, in fact, notorious for its frauds in respect of hagiography and relics as well as privileges (these things were very apt to go together) and its connexion with forgeries for Saint Ouen and St. Augustine's, Canterbury, is interesting and significant. If forgery had such cross-Channel ramifications in the twelfth century, a group of English religious houses making use of the same forged seal need cause no surprise. To know how and where they got it would be very interesting: perhaps from someone like Ansketil, who was caught out at St. Albans, or even from someone who had been connected with the royal Scriptorium.

Since accepted scriptores regis are found very suspiciously connected with the use of a forged royal seal, it is obvious that such criteria of authenticity as have been generally accepted for royal charters, writs, and seals cannot remain wholly unassailable. We may still be deceived by apparently genuine examples and there are some documents of which we are suspicious, but cannot be sure, beyond all reasonable doubt, that they are false. We do, however, believe that the accepted criteria of authenticity represent as high an order of probability as historians concerned with this period can well expect. Used with proper caution they are still indispensable in the study of charters and writs.

The great majority, however, of the texts of the charters and writs collected in the three preceding volumes of this series, covering the years 1066–1154, have survived, not as originals, but in later Chancery enrolments, cartulary copies, and official and unofficial transcripts of various kinds. These, if accurate and reliable, are just as good historical sources as originals, provided that we can be reasonably assured of their genuineness. The use of known forgeries as historical sources involves quite a different set of problems. We believe that no charter or writ should be condemned as spurious except on very positive grounds. Mere suspicion of irregularity is not enough to condemn, for we have read many documents which, on stylistic and formal diplomatic grounds, errors in dating, and so on, would be counted highly suspect had we not good evidence in the handwriting for believing them to be genuine products of scribes employed in the royal Scriptorium. Even so, there always remain such problems as those posed by the St. Martin's charters of Scriptor XIV, which we have already discussed. The text of every charter and writ, without exception, must be subjected to the most stringent possible historical criticism as well as to the tests for anachronism, while making allowance for the habit of many medieval scribes, when copying earlier documents, of extending superscriptions and other abbreviated matter in the style to which they themselves were best accustomed. We have also to contend (happily not very often in the work of contemporary scholars) with the very evil practice of 'normalizing' texts in transcripts and especially in print. Allowance must also be made for the fact that forgeries have often been embodied in perfectly genuine royal charters of confirmation and Letters Patent of Inspeximus: in other words, they were successful forgeries. Charters from these sources need to be considered on their merits, like all other texts. The vital question, then, arises of how far formal diplomatic can contribute to testing the authenticity of charters and writs of the Anglo-Norman kings.

For convenience of reference in the ensuing discussion we suggest the following orthodox analysis of the structure of Anglo-Norman royal charters and writs and nomenclature for their constituent parts:

I. THE INITIAL PROTOCOL

(a) The Superscription, i.e. the royal style and titles.

(b) The Address, which may be to an individual or a number of individuals or officials, to a shire or to the whole realm.[1]

(c) The Salutation, usually a simple *salutem*.

II. THE TEXT

(a) The Dispositive Clause, notifying (*sciatis*) that certain royal action has been taken, such as the making of a grant or confirmation.

(b) The Injunctive Clause (*Quare volo*, or the like) or, when the dispositive clause is omitted, beginning with *Precipio* or an equivalent, requiring the implementation of the royal will.

III. THE FINAL PROTOCOL

(a) A clause of 'Corroboration' or Authentication, such as *Sigilli mei impressione et auctoritate regia corroboro*, which is not regularly used in English royal charters and writs after the Conquest since it was not strictly necessary when these were duly attested and sealed.

(b) The Attestation by one or a number of witnesses, varying from a large number in important charters issued on solemn occasions to a single witness in certain types of writ. In witness-lists churchmen precede laymen and all are in due order of precedence according to the class of each witness and his status within it.

(c) The Chronological and Regnal Dates, also somewhat rare in Anglo-Norman documents.

(d) The Place-Date [(c) and (d) may be transposed].

IV. THE AUTHENTICATION

This is done by means of the king's seal, commonly appended on a tongue of parchment cut along the bottom of the document and left attached at the bottom left-hand corner by an inch or so of uncut parchment. These tongues, bearing the weight of the pendant seal in wax were very liable to get torn and quite a few surviving examples have been stitched up and a few have been folded lengthwise before sealing for additional strength. Occasionally a tag of parchment or leather passed through as slit or slits in a fold at the bottom of the document was used or, less

---

[1] Mr. Bishop and Dr. Chaplais (in *Facsimiles of English Royal Writs to A.D. 1100 Presented to Vivian Hunter Galbraith*) discuss the importance of the persons addressed in the Confessor's writs. In a new individual grant the address was special, but it was more general in a confirmation of a series of previous grants. This practice seems to have been continued after the Conquest, though scribes sometimes seem to be in considerable doubt about the address appropriate for a particular kind of document, since the old distinction was becoming increasingly difficult to make.

frequently in this age, cords similarly attached. When a tongue was used, it was customary to cut below it, at the very bottom of the document, a narrow strip also left attached at the bottom left-hand corner, to be used as a wrapper to tie up the writ or charter when it was folded in the shape of a small package with the seal hanging outside. In a legal sense the writ or charter was an appendage of the king's seal, not vice versa.

The fullest and most elaborate kind of writ-charter might contain every one of the elements we have enumerated; the briefest writ was bound to contain at least the initial protocol, with its superscription, address, and salutation, a text comprising an injunctive (occasionally only a dispositive) clause, a final protocol with attestation and place-date and the royal seal for authentication. It is possible that the degree of the document's elaboration may have depended, to some extent, upon what the beneficiary was prepared to pay but, generally speaking, the scribes of Henry I and Stephen, hard pressed as they were and scribbling away furiously, wasted neither parchment nor ink nor time.

The initial and final protocols are very formal and, as a rule, straightforward, but not so the dispositive and injunctive clauses of the text, which embody the meat of the document. It is here that scribes found most latitude for variation and idiosyncratic composition. These main clauses are susceptible of closer analysis and their constituent 'clausulae' may be noted. For example, either the dispositive or the injunctive clause, more usually the former and very seldom both, may include a 'movent' sub-clause setting out the formal, pious reasons, sometimes also the real ones, for the action taken or enjoined. The injunctive clause commonly includes an adverbial sub-clause descriptive, in formal, traditional, mnemonic terms, of the tenure of the liberties that go with the land or other property or rights, beginning usually with *bene et in pace et libere et quiete*. This may be done more or less elaborately in accordance with the requirements of law, but the trend was away from elaboration. The injunctive clause also commonly includes what might be called a 'locative' clausula, indicating in similar formal and traditional terms where the rights granted are to be exercised, such as *in bosco et in plano*, etc., which may, likewise, be elaborated or cut short with such a phase as *in omnibus aliis rebus et locis*. The injunctive clause often contains a short confirmatory sub-clause, such as *sicut carta regis Henrici testatur* or *sicut tenuerunt die qua rex Henricus fuit vivus et mortuus*. In certain types of writ, most commonly those concerning quittance of toll and custom, markets, fairs, etc., the injunctive clause ends with a sanction such as *super x libras forisfacture* or, in those concerned with seisin, *ne inde audiam clamorem pro defectu justicie* (or *penuria recti*), serious matters calling for the intervention of royal justice. Analysis of such a kind has been used ever since Mabillon set the study of diplomatic on a firm basis in his *De Re Diplomatica Libri Sex* (1681), but Mr. Bishop's *Scriptores Regis* (1961) has opened up new possibilities of study in the diplomatic of Anglo-Norman royal charters and writs. We have accepted with gratitude his identification by their handwriting of the scribes employed in Stephen's Scriptorium and we have adopted his numbering of them. In some cases we have ventured to disagree with Mr. Bishop about the dates when scribes were employed in the royal service. We have tried to identify the writers of a few charters and writs which were not included in his list though, since we are not experts in handwriting, we have done so subject to correction. Where we have expressed opinions at variance with Mr. Bishop's, we have done so with some diffidence.

The evidence available about these scribes shows that there were considerable fluctuations in the personnel of the royal Scriptorium and strongly suggests that the work of a scriptor regis was not confined to any particular aspect of a royal business. One hardly ventures to think of the royal household at this time as fully departmentalized and with separate scribal establishments. It has been doubted whether anything that could strictly be called a Chancery yet existed. We do not intend to enter into any argument about this, so we usually refer to the royal Scriptorium which, at least, is vouched for as an institution in *Constitutio Domus Regis*. Mr. Bishop has shown that Henry I's Scriptor VIII, besides writing royal charters and writs, wrote also a charter for Queen Matilda in favour of Durham and was the scribe of the Pipe Roll of 31 Henry I. Scriptor XIV's long career provides evidence, as do others, of the mobility of scribal labour, for he served Henry I, Stephen, the Empress, Archbishop Theobald, and Henry II. He also wrote a letter for Nigel Bishop of Ely and a charter for the Prior of Christchurch, Canterbury, in favour of Scriptor XIV himself. We believe that he also served St. Martin's le Grand, whether as a resident canon or as a scribal employee. Mr. Bishop has identified him with Peter the Scribe,[1] a person of some standing and property in Gloucester (which, before he sold it, may have drawn him to the side of the Empress). Similarly Scriptor XIII, after serving Henry I and Stephen, is found writing a charter for Robert de Sigillo Bishop of London, dated 1142,[2] which suggests that when he left the royal service, whether voluntarily or otherwise, he entered that of his former superior in the royal Scriptorium. It is possible that this connexion with Robert de Sigillo, once a monk of Reading, may bear upon Scriptor XIII's forged charter for Reading,[3] though abbot Reginald, once in Stephen's service, also falls under suspicion. One wonders whether scribes also entered the royal service through their employment by, or the patronage of, great officers of the Household and whether, for example, a change of chancellor involved a change in the staff of the Scriptorium. There are some indications that there may have been such a change on the fall of Roger the Chancellor in 1139, but the relevant charters cannot be dated closely enough to be sure of this.

We consider that the diplomatic structure of charters, writs, and *acta*, royal, episcopal, monastic, and baronial, reflects not only the requirements of law courts secular and ecclesiastical, royal, public, and private, but also the practices of a scribal profession whose members often moved from one employment to another. It may be that a place in the royal service was not necessarily the greatest plum, for its members were very hard-worked. It may not be without significance that such eminent men as Thomas Becket, his rival Roger de Pont l'Évêque, Archbishop of York, and John of Salisbury first made their mark (not necessarily as scribes) in the household of Theobald, Archbishop of Canterbury. Similarity of structure and phraseology is often very marked in the *acta* of various classes of men and many of the formulas are common currency in them all, when they deal with the same things, such as property and possession. This similarity has sometimes been attributed to the copying by lesser men of the *acta* of their betters. We think it is much better explained by other

---

[1] *Scriptores Regis*, 24–25 and plate xviib. See also *Regesta* iii, xiv.
[2] See Plate XI. [3] Plate X and *supra*.

causes. There can be little doubt that kings, prelates, many nobles, and at least some monasteries employed the same kind of professionally trained scribes, whose expertise played a very important part in evolving efficient ways of drafting documents to meet both administrative needs and the technical, legal requirements of the law courts. There were, naturally, differences in the drafting of the *acta* of various employers of scribal labour, not merely in superscriptions and forms of address. They had to be suited to the status and the kind of authority which the employer enjoyed. Phrases peculiarly appropriate to an episcopal charter and even its external appearance were not exactly suited to a royal or a baronial one. Consequently, when a royal scribe, such as XIII, sometimes introduces episcopal-sounding phrases or seems to echo the sonorous forms of the Courts Christian, it is relevant to consider whether he may not have gained his formative scribal experience in ecclesiastical rather than royal employment. Scriptor XIII, when he left the king's service, had no difficulty in producing a convincingly episcopal charter for the Bishop of London.[1]

A good scribe was literate not merely in the narrow sense. At least one of them, XXIII, who was in the service of Duke Henry, is described as *magister*. All had probably been trained in Rhetoric, if not formally in Law, were necessarily versed in the *Ars Dictaminis* and possessed the considerable administrative and technical knowledge that went to the correct drafting of a charter or other instrument. This must be obvious to anyone who studies the work of the hard-pressed scribes of Henry I and Stephen, whose incipiently cursive hands bear witness to the speed at which they had to write. Their quality varied but they were, in the main, a skilled and efficient body. It can, we believe, be seen from their drafting and the idiosyncrasies of their style that individual scriptores regis not merely copied or wrote from dictation but usually composed the documents they wrote, working within the framework of a well-known set of formulas. Sometimes a well-accented rhythm may be detected in the work of the best of them, though nothing quite comparable with the 'cursus' of the Papal Chancery.[2] We are inclined to judge from his variants that the unidentified scribe of the Exeter version of the 'Oxford Charter of Liberties' had a better sense of rhythm than the turgid Scriptor XIII, who wrote the Hereford version.[3]

The profession of scribe must have been an attractive one, with the chance, for its successful or fortunate members, of entering the service of a princely employer or a prelate, offering opportunities of gaining perquisites, emoluments, and promotion. In the rare cases where we learn the names and something of the circumstances of scribes, they appear to be men of some social standing and property.[4] Scribes must have been invaluable servants of kings and great men in church and state as makers and preservers of records, especially in an age of such turmoil, development, and change as the twelfth century was. The ablest and most ambitious might move from one employer to another whose service offered more attractive prospects; the unsuccessful must have eked out a living as best they could and probably were not averse to turning their talents to forgery, a very venial sin in the eyes of churchmen, if not of lawyers. Perhaps a scribe loyal to his employer might not be above forging on his behalf even without his knowledge. With the rapid growth in the twelfth century both

---

[1] Plate XI.

[2] See N. Denholm-Young, 'The Cursus in England', in *Collected Papers* (1947); C. R. Cheney, *English Bishops' Chanceries (1100–1250)* (1950).

[3] Plates IV and V.   [4] See, e.g., *Camden, 4th Ser., Miscellany xxii*, 14, no. 5.

of administration of all kinds and of the activation of the processes of law by the written word, went the growth and increasing expertise of the scribal profession—and, with these, increasing resort to forgery.

Léopold Delisle concluded from an elaborate study of the *acta* of Henry II that: 'ce qui frappe à la lecture des actes de Henri II c'est une rigoureuse fidélité à suivre un formulaire officiel, un emploi constant des mots propres, une régularité absolue dans la disposition des différents éléments de la pièce, une extrême concision, un abandon complet de tout ornement oiseux, une incomparable netteté dans les instructions et les ordres donnés.' We have not discerned quite such a rigorous regularity in the products of the royal Scriptorium in the reigns of Stephen and Henry I. The better scribes did, perhaps, strive to achieve a degree of regularity, simplicity of construction and precision in the expressions of the royal will which were embodied in the *acta* they composed. Within a broad framework royal scribes enjoyed a measure of latitude. They differ from one another as markedly in style as in handwriting, in draftsmanship, and the order in which they place the clausulae which constitute the texts of charters and writs. These documents, both in handwriting and in the details of their composition, are characterized, at one and the same time, by a remarkable homogeneity and by considerable permutations of their component parts. It will be seen that many of the originals, which we have reproduced in this volume, are marked by some quirks of style, vocabulary, or construction, or by errors or omissions or unusual additions. The earliest formularies that have survived date from the thirteenth century and we do not know from what kind of exemplars the scribes of Henry I and Stephen may have worked.

It would be tedious to examine here in detail the work of every individual scribe employed in Stephen's Scriptorium, but we hope that a brief study of a selected few will throw some light upon the diplomatic of our documents.

Of all the royal scribes, Scriptor XXII comes nearer than any of the others to fulfilling the specifications set out by Delisle. We can confidently say that none of his products is necessarily earlier than 1146 and he was still working in the royal Scriptorium in 1154, though it seems that neither he nor any of Stephen's scribes except Peter the Scribe (XIV) continued in the service of Henry II. Possibly the advent of Thomas Becket as Chancellor in January 1155 resulted in the replacement of the old staff of scribes. Peter, as a former servant of the Empress, may have had a stronger claim to favour.

It may be significant that such a relatively high degree of diplomatic uniformity as Scriptor XXII's products display was achieved only in the later years of Stephen's reign. This scribe's deliberate hand is matched by the drafting of his documents, which is most careful and methodical and shows a decided tendency to reduce the old mnemonic formulas to a minimum. For these reasons Scriptor XXII is at once the least interesting and the most important of Stephen's scribes, for he best exemplifies the trend towards standardization.

The superscription used by Scriptor XXII is *S. rex Angl* which, in fact, all the identified scriptores regis invariably use. The one outstanding exception and then in quite abnormal circumstances is in the 'Oxford Charter of Liberties' of 1136. So consistent is this practice that any other superscription in an original charter or writ of Stephen is a sure indication that it was not written by a royal scribe. Even the palaeographical variant *S. rex Angloy* is so very rare as to cause comment. This is not, however, to say that documents in which other superscriptions are used are necessarily forgeries, for charters were frequently written by beneficiaries' scribes and authenticated by the royal seal after, one would suppose, official scrutiny not so much of their diplomatic construction as of the accuracy of their contents. We think it likely that official scrutiny extended to documents presented for sealing no less than to those produced for royal confirmation, which were inspected and read *coram rege*, of which there is plenty of evidence.

Charters may bear what is often called a 'general' address, to archbishops, bishops, abbots, earls, and all the other categories of persons and officials in the realm who were of some account and who might be concerned in a jurisdictional or an official capacity. Writs and charters too, might be addressed to a shire, that is, to the bishop of the diocese, the earl, if there were one (but he was not invariably included), the royal justice, the sheriff, barons, and *fideles*; or to the justice, sheriff, and officials (*ministri*) of a shire; or to all within whose bailiwicks or spheres of jurisdiction and administration the beneficiary held lands; or to an individual or individuals, whether officials or others, sometimes to respondents in legal actions. The forms of address employed by Scriptor XXII are fairly consistent but by no means stereotyped in the twenty-three charters and writs he wrote for Stephen.[1] In his general addresses he tends to place earls after justices and occasionally he becomes very irregular, as in **151**, where the Archbishop of Canterbury is addressed with justices, earls, barons, sheriffs, etc., of England. It seems possible to discern the principle that specific individual grants, or confirmations of such, bear a shire address while more general confirmations bear a general address. If the rule was not invariably observed it was probably because of uncertainty on the part of the scribe, whose task was not always straightforward and uncomplicated, especially in drafting a multi-purpose document.

In composing dispositive clauses, Scriptor XXII is consistent in style and formulation, but the order in which he places the constituent *clausulae* is not stereotyped. In the dispositive clause he invariably uses *sciatis* with the accusative and infinitive construction, never other forms such as *sciatis quia* or *sciatis quoniam* with the perfect tense, which some scribes preferred. There appear to be three distinct variants in his wording:

1. *Sciatis me dedisse et concessisse*, which he uses for grants.
2. *Sciatis me concessisse et confirmasse* which is appropriate to confirmations.
3. *Sciatis me concessisse*, which seems to be reserved (quite logically) for quittances (**938**), licences (**258**), and the like.

Following such a notification, the main constituent parts of a dispositive clause commonly are:

(*a*) The name of the beneficiary.
(*b*) The thing granted, allowed or confirmed.
(*c*) Any further necessary details concerning the grant, etc.
(*d*) The nature of the tenure involved, whether in fee, frankalmoign, etc.
(*e*) A 'movent' giving the reasons, conventional or real, for the royal act.

---

[1] *Regesta* iii, xv. He wrote one (**243**) for the Queen.

Scriptor XXII uses these clausulae, or such of them as are necessary for the purpose in hand, in varying orders. This may be more a matter of style than of diplomatic draftsmanship, for it is difficult to see that any particular pattern is peculiarly fitted to a specific purpose.

So far, Scriptor XXII's handling of the clausulae of his charters and writs displays but a modest degree of uniformity. His injunctive clauses, on the other hand, embodying as they do explicit statements of the royal will and the most vital elements of the documents (if we bear in mind that every clausula mentioned below need not necessarily be included in every case) conform to an order that may fairly be called stereotyped. This would naturally have made it easier for those officially concerned with legal and administrative business to deal with Scriptor XXII's charters and writs quickly and efficiently. The main constituent clausulae of an injunctive clause generally are:

1. *Quare* (or *Et* or *Ideo*) *volo et precipio quod.*
2. The name of the beneficiary or a demonstrative pronoun (sometimes both are dispensed with and only the verb is used. The method of naming the beneficiary here is obviously superior to others.).
3. The thing(s) granted, allowed, confirmed, etc.
4. An adverbial clause, commonly *bene et in pace et libere*, etc.
5. Verb(s) of tenure, etc.
6. The nature of the tenure.
7. Mention of appurtenances and/or a 'locative' clausula, such as *in bosco et plano*, etc.
8. Mention of any associated franchises, customs, etc.
9. Mention of any quittances granted.
10. *Sicut unquam melius . . . tenuerunt* etc. or a similar phrase.
11. Sometimes a clause of protection or warranty.
12. Occasionally a 'movent'.

The regularity of Scriptor XXII's injunctive clauses and writs (*precipio*), which commonly take the same form, can be seen in all his products. The clausulae are regularly in the foregoing order, those that are unnecessary being omitted. Although the other scribes used the same clausulae similarly worded, they did not do so with anything like the same uniform order that Scriptor XXII employed; but the tendency was for this pattern to predominate. Did he stick closer than others to a formula or did he help to set a standard pattern in the royal Scriptorium?

Not only do we find considerable variations in the patterns of clausulae used by royal scribes, but the word-order and, within narrow limits, the vocabulary vary according to their sense of style and fitness. The texts of royal charters and writs, when examined in detail, show a good deal of variety and we cannot say that one form, such as that of Scriptor XXII, is right from the point of view of diplomatic and that the others are not; but it does seem to us that a significant trend towards uniformity can be discerned. It is some of Stephen's earlier scribes, especially Scriptor XIII, ever an individualist, who display the greater degree of irregularity and verbosity. None the less a warning must be uttered against the widely held belief that there was a standard 'Chancery pattern' for charters and writs from the very morrow of the

Norman Conquest and especially against the idea that it is possible confidently to read back from the writs of Glanvill's time to those of earlier days. It is better to try to trace the development as it occurred.

With regard specifically to writs, there are problems relating both to their nomenclature and to their legal significance. When, as is the case more often than not, we cannot give them precise legal names in the pre-Glanvill age, how are we to describe them? In a previous volume of this series the then editors adopted what was perhaps a naïve nomenclature, giving the name 'precept' to writs which used the word *precipio* and 'mandate' to those which employed the word *mando*. This left out of account those which began *volo* or *volo et mando*, which could hardly have been called 'volitives'. It may prove more satisfactory, at least till our knowledge of early writs is more precise, to distinguish writ (*precipio*), writ (*mando*), writ (*volo*), etc. It is difficult to discern a clear principle regulating the use of these different imperative verbs, or the practical distinction, if any, that is intended. We have never noticed *jubeo* in a royal charter or writ, though it is used in those of some magnates, e.g. Rannulf, Earl of Chester. A Gloucester Abbey charter (**350**) contains the phrase *et prohibeo ne inde placitent . . . pro aliquo brevi vel precepto*, which would lead us to suppose that there was a distinction between a writ and a 'precept'; perhaps that the latter might be delivered orally by a royal (or other) representative.

There are writs which begin with a direct imperative; e.g. *Redde festinanter monachis de Ely allecia sua*.[1] There are variants of the writ (*precipio*) type which begin with a conditional clause: e.g. *Si canonici Sancti Martini Londoniensis poterint monstrare . . . tunc precipio quod illos faciatis resaisiri . . . .*[2] In this case a royal reeve is ordered to deal with a complaint of disseisin. Some writs of the *precipio* type, because of their nature, bear a very close resemblance to an ordinary injunctive clause; others do not resemble this at all. It is difficult to discern a principle which determines the inclusion or omission of a dispositive clause in writs. Two writs may be addressed in exactly the same way, e.g. for a shire, and may appear to deal with closely analogous matters, yet one is drafted with both dispositive and injunctive clauses, the other simply in injunctive form. It may be that such seeming inconsistencies reflect the slow evolution of legal writs, or that the two forms represent administrative or legal niceties or steps in litigation with which we are not familiar.

Several writs of the *precipio* type, resembling closely in form the ordinary injunctive clause, are in the hand of Scriptor XXII.[3] What strikes one about these is that the order of the clausulae, while quite consistent, differs from that used by the same scribe in the injunctive clauses of his writ-charters. While other scribes are less consistently rigid in the drafting of such writs, it is worth noticing that Scriptor XXII's pattern occurs more frequently than others. It seems to us significant that Scriptor XXII was so meticulous in the drafting of the injunctive parts of his charters and writs. He seems to have appreciated the value and convenience of uniformity and probably the importance of the legal construction that would be placed upon what he wrote when he formally expressed the royal will in any matter.

One of the more puzzling documents of the writ (*precipio*) type is in favour of

---

[1] **260**. Plate XII *a*.
[2] **545**. This writ is in the hand which we believe to be that of Scriptor XIV, not of an imitator.
[3] **146, 471, 488, 670**.

Durham Cathedral, written in the hand of Scriptor XIV (255). It is difficult to see why this, which bears a 'general' address (abbots omitted) and has four witnesses, should not have a dispositive as well as an injunctive clause, like an ordinary writ-charter. The great majority of writs of the *precipio* type are addressed to shires—bishop, (earl), royal justice, sheriff, barons, officials (*ministri*), and lieges (*fideles*)—or to all justices, sheriffs, and officials in whose bailiwicks the beneficiary holds lands. As a rule these are attested by a single witness or occasionally two, who are often quite undistinguished members of the royal household, such as under-chamberlains. This is why the Durham example seems so unusual. Again, some of these writs consist of two or more distinct parts dealing with two or more matters. No. **525**, for example, is in favour of Roger of Salisbury and his canons of St. Martin le Grand. It first confirms him in possession of their lands (probably a preliminary that was legally necessary) and then orders him to be reseised of those lands that had been taken from them following the arrest of the Bishops in 1139. Here the two parts of the writ are obviously and closely connected, but this was not always so clearly the case. A considerable number of royal writs of the period are multi-purpose documents and therefore very difficult to categorize. Another St. Martin's writ in the hand of Scriptor XXI and addressed to Geoffrey Pietas (**537**) is a case in point. Are we to regard this technically as a writ for execution of judgment (*quia vidi et audivi cartam regis Henrici*)? But it also includes an injunction, of a kind which developed into the writ *Ne injuste vexes*,[1] a *ne intromittas*, an order for payment of tithes and an admonitory *ne super hoc audiam inde clamorem* which, in default of obedience, should have brought royal justice into action. Doubtless all this hangs together, but it is a complex affair. Yet another St. Martin's writ in the hand of Scriptor XIV, addressed to Geoffrey de Mandeville (**543**) might also be regarded as a writ for execution of judgment, but the circumstances seem to have required a diplomatic structure different from the last-mentioned writ, namely, a straightforward instruction to give the canons of St. Martin's seisin of specified lands. The writ, already quoted, in favour of the monks of Ely Cathedral Priory, in the hand of Scriptor XIV, addressed to the reeve of Dunwich,[2] might be classed as a Writ of Right because it includes the words: *Et plenam justitiam eis inde facias . . . ne quicquam amittant pro penuria justitie*, or as a Writ of Debt.

A writ in favour of Durham Cathedral, in the hand of Scriptor XIII, which is addressed to R. and his sister O. de Muschamps (**257**) might represent a stage in the evolution of the *Writ of Novel Disseisin* (though, in form, it is far from the classical writ of that name) or a stage in the evolution of legal procedure in such an action. It includes a not uncommon clause: *Et nisi feceritis Eustachius filius Johannis faciat, ne inde audiam clamorem*, which suggests execution of judgement. In many such writs the ultimate sanction was action by the royal justice of the shire to implement the king's command. The diplomatic structure of writs of this kind seems to have been well established. They take the following form:

1. Address to the disseisor(s).
2. Order to restore possession.
3. To a named complainant.

---

[1] *Glanvill*, ed. Woodbine, xii. 10, pp. 152-3.   [2] **260** and Plate XII *a*.

4. Of specific land, etc.
5. In a specified manner—e.g. as the complainant had best and most freely held it at a specified time.
6. A sanction: *nisi feceris N* (commonly the royal justice of the shire) *faciat*.
7. *Ne inde audiam clamorem*, etc.

Attention needs also to be drawn to writs cast in a different diplomatic mould. They are often in the form: *Precipio ut N. teneat*; while others say *Precipio tibi quod permittas N. tenere* (**537**). Yet others are in the form of an imperative more or less minatory: *Sicut me amas et ea que de me tenes, precipio tibi quod infra tertium diem postquam hoc breve meum videris, eas ad Sanctum Martinum Londonie et sicut tibi dixi fidelitatem facias . . .* (**539**) or *Mando vobis et precipio quod computetis . . .* in a writ of the Empress to the Barons of the Exchequer (**628**. Cf. **631**). Some of these, if genuine, seem to be of a kind which developed into standard administrative writs or legal 'writs of course'; others are so much affairs of the moment that we cannot expect them to be in a stereotyped form. Considerable numbers of writs of the Norman kings remain to puzzle the student of diplomatic and the legal historian. Until the precise nature and administrative or legal function of a writ have been established, diplomatic can neither elucidate its structure nor pronounce confidently upon its genuineness.

Our examination of the scribal habits of Scriptor XXII has led us to consider the structure of charters and writs of the pre-Glanvill era and some of the problems connected with them. An examination of the work of a small sample of the other *scriptores regis* in Stephen's employment may, we hope, be of some value for comparative purposes.

First, we take Scriptor XIII because he was by far the most idiosyncratic of all the scribes who served Henry I and Stephen. His style seems to us to be that of a Continental rather than an English scribe and it has a strong ecclesiastical tinge. Mr. Bishop has called his hand 'awkward and insensitive'; the drafting of his documents shows the utmost freedom and such inflated formulation as appears in few other originals written by royal scribes. The confirmatory clausulae in a charter of Henry I in favour of St. Mary of Fontevrault[1] are a good example of his florid style which, indeed, caused the editors of *Regesta* ii, who had not the advantage of knowing him by his handwriting as a royal scribe, to entertain some suspicions about this charter. '*Hanc itaque meam donationem factam anno M°c°xxx° ab incarnatione domini, confirmatam precibus meis ab auctoritate domini et beate memorie Innocentii pape, summi pontificis, collaudatam et approbatam ab episcopis baronibus et personis regni mei et Normannie, ego Henricus facio, factam collaudo, collaudatam confirmo, confirmatam regia potestate et a deo mihi collata auctoritate illi ecclesie in perpetuum obtinendam integram inconcussamque corroboro et testimonio presentis scripti sigilligue mei consigno*' is excessively inflated and pontifical for a royal charter. Grandiose and pretentiously ecclesiastical drafting of this kind is what Scriptor XIII delighted and indulged in at the slightest opportunity. Several of the scribe's other charters, one, for example, in favour of Beverley Minster,[2] would undoubtedly be suspect on the ground of their inflated formulation if they were not written in the hand identified as

---

[1] *Regesta* ii, ccxlviii.   [2] **99** and Plate VI.

that of a prolific royal scribe. The fact that Scriptor XIII's handwriting appears in a Reading Abbey charter with a fragment of the forged First Seal of Stephen on the tongue (Plate X) does not strengthen our confidence in his products. In the Beverley charter the 'general' address is in an unusually shortened form. The dispositive clause opens with the phrase *presentis carte attestatione confirmo*, an unusual gambit in a royal charter of this date and there is a characteristically elaborate corroborative clause which, though not very often used by royal scribes, is paralleled by, for example, Scriptores XIX, XXI, and even XXII.[1] Even in something so simple as a 'general' address, Scriptor XIII is capable of introducing wording which is incongruous in a royal charter, such as *baronibus et omnibus filiis sancte ecclesie per Angliam et Normanniam constitutis*,[2] with its strongly ecclesiastical tone.

In his dispositive and injunctive clauses Scriptor XIII makes little, if any, effort to maintain a consistent sequence of clausulae and, unlike many of the royal scribes, he does not regularly use the same grammatical constructions for the same purposes. He may begin a dispositive clause with *sciatis* followed by accusative and infinitive (**166, 679**) or with *sciatis quia* or *sciatis quoniam* with the perfect tense (**800**). He could indeed write a royal injunction in very concise and peremptory terms (**143, 257**), yet a concise writ in favour of Lewes Priory includes a characteristically elaborate and clumsy turn of phrase: *Et super hoc non patiamini quod aliquid distrahatur ab ea quod ab antiquo habere solebat et habere juste debeat.*[3] A study of Scriptor XIII's documents quickly reveals his style and rhythm; e.g. *confírmo ecclésie Sáncti Johánnis de Beverláco pácem súam ínfra leúgam súam et ejúsdem violáte pácis emendatiónem sícut est a rége Alestáno ípsi ecclésie colláta et a céteris Anglórum régibus confirmáta.*[4] He seems to pride himself on the cadences which may reflect a scribal apprenticeship in ecclesiastical employment.

What of the charter for Reading Abbey which bears an identifiable fragment of the forged First Seal of Stephen (Plate X)? For Scriptor XIII this is, in formulation, a most restrained document. There is little to excite remark as far as its diplomatic structure is concerned; it is as commonplace a royal confirmation as we have ever set eyes upon and might well stand as a model for such charters. It is as if Scriptor XIII deliberately set himself to compose a run-of-the-mill product of the royal Scriptorium for this particular purpose, rather than a charter in his own inflated style. It remains as a solemn warning against reliance upon diplomatic criteria alone to determine the authenticity of royal charters and writs of this period.

Scriptor XIV is of some interest, both because he was in the service successively of Henry I, Stephen, the Empress, probably St. Martin's le Grand, Archbishop Theobald, and Henry II and because Mr. Bishop has identified him with Peter the Scribe.[5] He is only moderately consistent in his draftsmanship though he is a businesslike scribe. His work displays no very marked individuality and his vocabulary is thoroughly conventional. Scriptor XIV, in fact, contrasts markedly with Scriptor XIII. In dispositive clauses he shows a consistent preference for *sciatis* with accusative and infinitive. Only once does he depart from this construction, namely, in the first charter of the Empress for Geoffrey de Mandeville.[6] There he writes *sciant omnes tam*

---

[1] **69, 538, 103.**

[2] *Regesta* ii, cclxx (where an incorrect text was derived from P.R.O. Transcripts 8|140 B. II, p. 4). The original (Arch. de l'Eure, H. 4033) is slightly mutilated.

[3] *Regesta* ii, lv.   [4] Plate VI.   [5] *Scriptores Regis*, plate xviib.   [6] **274** and Plate XIV.

presentes quam futuri quod ego M. regis Henrici filia et Anglorum domina . . . . This is not
at all the customary formula in other charters of the Empress or of any of the Norman
kings but rather what might be expected in a private charter. Having, strangely,
omitted the title *Anglorum domina* from the superscription, Scriptor XIV apparently
tries to repair the omission here in the dispositive clause, virtually beginning the
charter afresh. Perhaps so very marked a departure from the regal norm was due both
to the unusual circumstances in which the Empress was placed at the time and to the
nature of the document which is much more like a detailed agreement or 'final
concord' than an ordinary royal charter. For the rest, we can only remark upon
trifling points in Scriptor XIV's work. He consistently writes *rex Henricus* not
Henricus rex, as many other scribes do. Small points of this kind can be picked out
in the work of every scribe and perhaps a sufficiently detailed study, with the aid of a
computer, would enable us to assign to their original scribes charters and writs which
we know only from enrolments, cartularies, and transcripts. Very occasionally an
emphatic phrase stands out from the flat level of Scriptor XIV's compositions: *Precipio quod sine dilatione facias resaisiri ecclesiam et canonicos Sancti Martini . . . ita
plenarie dico facias eos resaisiri sicut inde saisiti fuerunt, ipsi et ecclesia sua, die qua
dedi manerium illud* (**543**). This reads like a very emphatic oral order faithfully
reproduced.

   Scriptor XIX is also of some interest for, although the extant examples of his work
are not numerous, several of the charters he wrote are intrinsically important. One
charter creates Geoffrey de Mandeville Earl of Essex (**273**) and another confers upon
Robert, Earl of Leicester, the earldom of Hereford (Plate XXV). These two charters
are somewhat similar in external appearance though the seals are appended differently,
and their texts differ in almost every detail. The first, however, is a new creation; the
other grants a second earldom to the beneficiary. Another charter written by Scriptor
XIX in favour of the Hospital of Beaulieu de Chartres (**69**) attracts our attention
because it embodies a 'liberate': *Et ipsis thesaurariis meis precipio ut eas eis omni
anno ad terminum predictum sine omni disturbatione et occasione liberent.* This whole
document is something of a hybrid. Ostensibly it is a confirmation of Henry I's grant
of £10 per annum from the Treasury, but in diplomatic structure it is neither a
straightforward writ-charter nor a simple writ (*precipio*). It begins with a dispositive
clause and ends with a long list of witnesses together with the relatively rare calendar
and regnal dates. It is to be observed that both *Rogero cancellario* in the list of witnesses and the calendar date are written over erasures. There is also a clause of
authentication strongly reminiscent of Scriptor XIII: *hanc . . . illi et fratribus infirmis
sine fine mansuram regia auctoritate corroboro et a deo mihi collata potestate inviolatam
permanere confirmo et presentis sigilli mei impressione constituo.* The whole document is redolent of administrative confusion, combining a charter of confirmation
with a 'liberate' writ for the royal or ducal Treasurers, but true neither to the one
form nor to the other.

   The work of the scriptores regis seems to show that a degree of latitude was taken
for granted in the drafting of royal charters and writs. Rigid adherence to highly
stereotyped forms was not characteristic of them. Comparison with other scriptores
shows that they all employed a common technical vocabulary and phraseology with
variations to suit the *acta* of different kinds of employers. These were the vocabulary

and phraseology of their profession determined by the requirements of the law courts and of administration. The royal scribes worked within a framework that was still flexible. The age of the Norman kings and especially the first half of the twelfth century saw considerable developments in the drafting of charters and writs to meet changing needs. There was a tendency to reduce the old, traditional, mnemonic phrases to more concise forms and newer formulas were coming gradually to be used as administrative and legal procedure evolved. While the work of the royal scribes shows homogeneity and regularity, their products fell far short of the much more stereotyped forms which can be seen in and after Henry II's reign. We think that such a degree of stereotyping could not have been achieved earlier, partly because administrative techniques were not yet sufficiently advanced, partly because of the continuing uncertainties of the law to which the author of *Leges Henrici Primi* bore witness and to which the disturbances of Stephen's reign must have added yet more uncertainty. The great change came as a result of the working, in the spheres of law and administration, of that reforming genius which has been traditionally associated with the reign of Henry II and also with a royal household machine increasingly well organized and departmentalized. Given this, the scriptores regis quickly adapted the documents they wrote to meet the new requirements of the legal situation and the administrative needs of the new age.

Of the men who wrote the original charters and writs of Stephen which have survived, a number can be identified as scriptores regis by their handwriting. In so far as we have attempted to follow in Mr. Bishop's footsteps by identifying scriptores, we have found that his principles and his indications of individuality in handwriting seem to work satisfactorily. We believe, as he does, that a sufficient number (necessarily indefinite) of royal charters and writs in the same handwriting, issued for different beneficiaries on different occasions, is a reasonably reliable indication that they are the work of a royal scribe, especially if some of them bear genuine seals. But we have shown that there are serious exceptions to the rule. A good many scribes are 'unidentified', and this in several senses. Some are 'unidentified' because we have not enough and sufficiently varied examples of their work to be reasonably sure whether or not they are royal scribes. Of others it may be said that, because all the surviving originals in their handwriting are in favour of one beneficiary, they cannot be 'identified' as royal scribes and must be regarded as probably employed by the beneficiary. In the case of yet other scribes it seems clear from their stiff and formal handwriting and their clumsy draftsmanship that they were not royal, or even professional, scriptores.

The royal scribes of Henry I and Stephen made increasing use of cursive handwriting because they had so much to do that they were forced to write quickly to keep up with the work. Scribes not in royal employment were probably not under anything like the same pressure; though here we ought perhaps to make an exception of those who served great administrators like Roger Bishop of Salisbury (Plates XLVIII, XLIX, L) and some of the busier prelates. Such scribes often wrote a more leisurely hand than the scriptores regis, when they were employed by beneficiaries to write charters which were to be authenticated by the royal seal.

We think that a basic distinction is to be made between trained professional scriptores, who had the necessary skill to draft legal and administrative documents of whatever kind, and scribes who were employed simply because their services were readily and gratuitously available, as in a monastic cloister, but who were obviously much more at home in writing or copying liturgical or literary manuscripts than official *acta*. The draftsmanship of such scribes is often clumsy, old fashioned, and prone to anachronism.[1] Perhaps they had to seek exemplars in such previous charters as were available and these must sometimes have been poor guides to current practice. The products of such scribes are not difficult to detect but, with all their technical faults, it is dangerous to assert that they are fabricated unless there is very clear evidence of an historical kind that the claims they embody are false.

To distinguish (when we do not possess the originals) between the work of scriptores regis and that of other professional scriptores employed by beneficiaries is much more difficult. Both in external appearance and in draftsmanship the charters written by the latter show a professional competence as great as that of any royal scribe. A good professional scriptor was bound to be versed in the drafting of *acta* of whatever kind his employment might require him to write. He could probably turn his hand equally well to an episcopal or baronial charter, a chirograph, a royal writ, or even a Pipe Roll or an estates survey. No doubt long service in a particular employment, such as that of a bishop, especially in his formative years, left its mark indelibly on his style and draftsmanship; but such professional scriptores, if they turned to forgery, would be difficult to detect. On the other hand we must always remember that some of the scriptores regis were capable of inflated formulation, confused drafting, careless mistakes, and even, it would seem, forgery.

For reasons such as these we doubt whether it is possible by diplomatic criteria *alone*, useful though they are, to distinguish in every case the products of the royal Scriptorium, in the period with which we are concerned, from those of professional scriptores who were not in the royal service. Neither do we think that diplomatic criteria alone can enable us to pronounce with confidence upon the authenticity of royal charters and writs of this period which are known only from enrolments, cartularies, and transcripts. It is possible to make certain value-judgements on such a basis, such as, 'this is a well-drafted charter which accords with the practices of identified scriptores regis', but this is no sure guarantee of authenticity; or, 'this is a badly drafted charter, full of faults and anachronisms, which could hardly have been written by a scriptor regis', but this is not an infallible indication that it is a forgery. There is need for a wider study of scribal habits, which should not be limited to royal documents.

Since formal charters and writs and, more specifically, writs of direct legal significance were more likely than ephemeral administrative writs to survive from the age before the Chancery enrolments began, we have many of the legal and relatively few of the purely administrative type. Till legal historians have made us more familiar with the details of legal procedure in the pre-Glanvill age, it will be difficult to establish firmly the exact purpose and significance of a good many writs. Only when these are established will it be possible to compile the section on the writs of the Norman kings for that *Manual of English Diplomatic* for which Professor T. F. T. Plucknett pleaded in his Presidential Address to the Royal Historical Society in 1949.[2]

We have reproduced a few of the *acta* of the Empress and a number of those of

---

[1] For an extreme example see Plate XLII.   [2] *T.R.H.S.* 4th Series, xxxii (1950), 151.

Duke Henry, but only two of Duke Geoffrey, and we have commented upon these individually in our notes on the plates. Duke Geoffrey's surviving original charters for Normandy are not numerous. A study of these would have involved a comparative study of his charters for Anjou. Although we have not been able to undertake this, it seems to us quite evident that his charters for Normandy are strongly in the Norman tradition. This is not surprising since Geoffrey was careful to retain the services of a Norman chancellor for Normandy.[1] His documents, in external appearance and in composition suggest (what was in fact the case) that Geoffrey took over the administration of Normandy as a going concern.

Most of the charters of the Empress are less official-looking than those of her husband and son and are in marked contrast with those of Stephen. Many of Stephen's surviving original charters and writs are written in a 'court' hand by identifiable royal scribes; those of the Empress are more often written in a 'book' hand by the beneficiaries' scribes. Stephen's documents are generally brief, efficient, and to the point, looking as if the scribes had dashed them off without waste of time or material. The charters of the Empress are more lengthy affairs written on great wide pieces of parchment and rather painstakingly composed. Even charters written for her by such an experienced ex-royal scriptor as XIV (Peter the Scribe) were not always in the tradition of the royal Scriptorium,[2] mainly because of the peculiar circumstances of these grants.

King Stephen's seal has an obverse and a reverse[3] and is usually, but not invariably, appended on a tongue; that of the Empress has an obverse only,[4] gives her no English title and is often attached by a tag, thong, or cords.

The charters of the Empress are, we think, for these reasons, much less significant for the study of English diplomatic than those of King Stephen and Duke Henry. Henry's English charters prior to his accession to the throne are clearly the product of his own ducal scriptorium. Although their external appearance is regular, we have the impression that those which concern England were drafted by scribes who were still learning the English way of doing things. They were not dashed off like the products of Stephen's scribes and, although their drafting is, in many respects, normal, unfamiliarity with English ways is shown in many details and the authentic regal touch is sometimes lacking. Thus, in Henry's charter for Biddlesden (Plate XL *a*) rights and liberties which should normally be enumerated in the dispositive clause are mentioned in the injunctive clause only. The tenor of the confirmation for Nigel fitz Arthur (Plate XL *b*) is more suggestive of a baron dealing with a sub-tenant than of a quasi-regal act. In Plate XLI it will be seen that the beneficiary is described as *familiari et dilecto amico meo*, which is very unusual in an English royal charter of this date and the injunctive clause consists simply of the order *ne quis inde injuriam aliquam faciat*. The instinct of these scribes was for brevity. Henry's seal was usually on a tongue and resembled a royal seal, as did his father's. The intermingling of the English and the Angevin-Norman traditions in the court, administration, and scriptorium of Henry II were of vital importance for the future.

---

[1] See Plates XXXVIII and XXXIX.   [2] See Plate XIV.   [3] See Plates I and II.
[4] See Plate XIII.

LIST OF PLATES

LOCATION OF THE ORIGINAL CHARTERS
AND WRITS OF KING STEPHEN, QUEEN MATILDA, THE EMPRESS MATILDA, AND DUKES GEOFFREY AND HENRY

Notes

1. Archives or Libraries are listed alphabetically, but private owners of individual charters are listed at the end, with the owners' address as correct in March 1968.

2. In column 3 the Roman numerals refer to the *scriptores regis* identified by T. A. M. Bishop and discussed in *Regesta* iii, pp. xiii–xv. The letters in this column refer to private scribes whose hands have been detected in more than one charter. They can be listed as follows:

Scribe **a**: **309, 310, 999.**
Scribe **b**: **928, 929, 939.**
Scribe **c**: **313, 787, 788.**
Scribe **d** (identified by Bishop as the 'imitator' of scriptor **xiv**): **539, 540, 545, 547, 549, 552, 558, 559.**
Scribe **e**: **626, 627.**
Scribe **f**: **629, 632,** and possibly **115, 116.**
Scribe **g**: **306, 492.**
Scribe **h**: **77, 443.**

3. In column 4, the abbreviations used for the grantors are as follows:

   G Duke Geoffrey
 GH Duke Geoffrey and his son (Duke) Henry
   H Duke Henry
 (H) Attestation by Duke Henry
   M The Empress Matilda
 MH The Empress and her son (Duke) Henry
 QM Queen Matilda
  RS Bishop Roger of Salisbury (as Justiciar)
   S King Stephen

Archive or Library	Reference	Scriptor	Grantor	Number in Regesta, vol. iii	Plate in Regesta, vol. iv
Belvoir Castle, Lincs.	Acle no. 669	xx	S	176	xxviii b
,, ,,	Royal Grant no. 479	xiii	S	716	vii
Berkeley Castle, Glos.	..	a	H	309	
,, ,,	..	a	H	310	
,, ,,	..	a	H	999	
,, ,,	..	xxiii?	H	1000	
Beverley Corporation Archives	No. 2, Schedule 1	xiii	S	99	vi
Burton-on-Trent, Municipal Offices	Anglesea Charters	xviii	S	135	
Calvados, Archives du, Caen	2 D 12	xiii	S	749	
,, ,,	H 5603	?	H	326	
,, ,,	H 6518	?	M	748	
Cambridge, Jesus College	..	xxii	S	138	
,, ,,	..	xxii	S	139	
Cambridge, King's College	B. 7a	?	S	118	
,, ,,	Dd. 17	?	(H)	80	
,, ,,	2.W.1	xiv	M	651	xv
Cambridge, University Library, *see* Ely					
Canterbury Cathedral Library	Ch. B. 335	xxii	S	151	
,, ,,	Ch. C. 11	xiii	S	143	
,, ,,	Ch. C. 12	xxi	S	145	
,, ,,	Ch. C. 13	xxii	S	146	
,, ,,	Ch. D. 6	xxii	S	150	
,, ,,	Ch. S. 312	xxi	S	147	
,, ,,	Ch. S. 314	xxii	S	148	
,, ,,	Ch. X. 10	?	QM	149	
Chichester City Archives	A/1	?	S	181	
Durham, the Prior's Kitchen	1. 1. Reg. 13	xiv	S	255	
,, ,,	1. 1. Reg. 14	xiv	S	256	
,, ,,	1. 1. Reg. 15	xiii	S	257	
,, ,,	1. 1. Reg. 16	xxii	S	258	
,, ,,	1. 4. Ebor. 3	xx	S	835	
Ely, Dean and Chapter Muniments (in Cambridge University Library)	Ch. 7	?	S	262	xliv
,, ,,	Ch. 8	xx	S	266	xxvii b
,, ,,	Ch. 8 b	xiv	S	260	xii a
Essex Record Office, Chelmsford	D/DP, T1/273	xxi	S	877	
Eure, Archives de l', Évreux	H. 438	xxiv	S	495	
,, ,,	H. 438 (bis)	xxiv	S	495	
,, ,,	H (Supplément) Bec	xix	S	74	xxvi
Eure-et-Loire, Archives de l', Chartres	G. 2984	xix	S	69	
,, ,,	G. 2984	?	M	71	
,, ,,	G. 2984	?	MH	72	
Exeter Cathedral Library	2073	?	S	284	xlii
,, ,,	2529	?	S	271	iv
Gloucester Cathedral	St. Peter's Abbey Deeds, vol. vi, f. 12	xxii	S	360	xxxiv a
Gloucestershire Records Office, Gloucester	D 471/T1/2	g	H	306	xl b
Hertfordshire County Record Office, Hertford	AS. 1	xiii	S	679	x
Keele University Library	Hatton Wood Coll. 708	xviii	S	963	xxiii
Lincoln Cathedral Muniments	A1/1/6	xxii	S	488	
,, ,,	A1/1/7	xxi	S	485	
,, ,,	A1/1/8	xxii	S	486	
,, ,,	A1/1/9	xxii	S	471	
,, ,,	A1/1/10	xxi	S	484	
,, ,,	A1/1/40	g	H	492	
London, British Museum	Add. Ch. 5861	xxii	S	669	
,, ,,	Add. Ch. 19576	?	M	699	
,, ,,	Add. Ch. 19577	?	M	703	
,, ,,	Add. Ch. 19578	?	M	697	
,, ,,	Add. Ch. 19579	?	M	703	xlvi
,, ,,	Add. Ch. 19580	xiii	S	688	viii b
,, ,,	Add. Ch. 19581	xxi	S	694	
,, ,,	Add. Ch. 19582	xxi	S	689	xxxiii
,, ,,	Add. Ch. 19583	?	S	692	
,, ,,	Add. Ch. 19584	xviii	S	690	xxii
,, ,,	Add. Ch. 20420	f?	M	115	
,, ,,	Add. Ch. 28315	xiv	S	40	
,, ,,	Add. Ch. 28316	xvi	S	39	
,, ,,	Add. Ch. 28317	xx	S	42	

Archive or Library	Reference	Scriptor	Grantor	Number in Regesta, vol. iii	Plate in Regesta, vol. iv
London, British Museum (*cont.*)	Add. Ch. 28318	xx	S	41	
,, ,,	Add. Ch. 28319	xx	S	318	
,, ,,	Add. Ch. 28320	?	S	374	
,, ,,	Campbell Ch. xiv. 6	xxii	S	519	
,, ,,	Campbell Ch. xxix. 3	?	S	201	
,, ,,	Campbell Ch. xxix. 8	xxi	S	873	
,, ,,	Cotton Ch. vii. 4	xix	S	273	
,, ,,	Cotton Ch. xvi. 27	xiv	M	274	xiv
,, ,,	Cotton Ch. xvi. 34	xvi	S	500	xviii
,, ,,	Cotton Ch. xvi. 35	?	QM	503	
,, ,,	Cotton Ch. xvii. 2	xxiii	H	180	
,, ,,	Cotton MS. Nero C. 3, f. 177	xiii	S	132	ix
,, ,,	Egerton Ch. 2213	xx	S	308	
,, ,,	Harl. Ch. 43 C. 13	xviii	S	114	xxiv
,, ,,	Harl. Ch. 83 A. 24	?	S	814	
,, ,,	Harl Ch. 84 C. 2	xxii	S	103	
,, ,,	Harl. Ch. 84 C. 3	xxiii	H	104	xl a
,, ,,	Loans 29/242/14	xxii	S	336	
London, Public Record Office	DL/10/9	xxi	S	179	
,, ,,	DL/10/11	xiv	S	388	xii b
,, ,,	DL/10/12	xvii	S	389	xix
,, ,,	DL/10/13	xx	S	390	xxvii a
,, ,,	DL/10/14	xix	S	437	xxv
,, ,,	DL/10/15	xx	S	493	
,, ,,	DL/10/16	xiv	M	392	
,, ,,	DL/10/17	xiv	M	394	xiii
,, ,,	DL/10/18	xx	S	276	
,, ,,	DL/10/19	xiv	M	111	
,, ,,	DL/10/20	xviii	S	312	xxi
,, ,,	DL/10/21	xxii	S	317	
,, ,,	DL/10/22	xxii	QM	243	
,, ,,	DL/25/2	c	RS	313	l
,, ,,	E 40/1042	xxi	S	510	
,, ,,	E 40/1051	xxi	S	508	
,, ,,	E 40/2021	xxii	S	515	xxxvii
,, ,,	E 40/3081	xx	S	668	
,, ,,	E 40/5276	?	S	960	
,, ,,	E 40/5420	xxi	S	244	
,, ,,	E 40/5938	xxiii	H	339	
,, ,,	E 40/6683	xxi	S	507	xxxii
,, ,,	E 40/6688	?	M	518	
,, ,,	E 40/6691	xxii	S	450	xxxv b
,, ,,	E 40/6987	xx	S	517	xxviii a
,, ,,	E 40/14890	?	S	516	xlv b
,, ,,	E 40/14897	xxii	S	504	xxxvi
,, ,,	E 40/14898	xviii	S	579	
,, ,,	E 40/14899	xiv	S	15	
,, ,,	E 40/14900	xxii	S	670	
,, ,,	E 40/15389	xxii	S	448	xxxiv b
,, ,,	E 40/15394	?	S	446	xlv a
,, ,,	E 40/15395	xvii	S	445	xx b
,, ,,	E 40/15443	xxii	S	449	xxxv a
,, ,,	E 40/15911	b	S	929	
,, ,,	E 42/309	?	S	499	
,, ,,	E 326/11342	d	S	545	
,, ,,	E 326/11348	xviii	S	667	
,, ,,	E 327/254	xxi	S	177	xxix b
London, Robinson Trust, 8 Waterloo Place, S.W.1	..	?	S	288	
London, St. Paul's Cathedral Library	A 60/36	?	S	562	xliii a
,, ,,	A 40/1443	xiii	..	..	xi
London, Westminster Abbey Muniments	968*	d	QM	539	
,, ,,	1111	d	S	540	
,, ,,	1112	d	S	559	
,, ,,	1114	xxi	S	538	
,, ,,	1120	xxi	S	537	
,, ,,	1137	d	S	552	
,, ,,	8110	d	S	549	xvii
,, ,,	8111	xiv	S	543	

Archive or Library	Reference	Scriptor	Grantor	Number in Regesta, vol. iii	Plate in Regesta, vol. iv
London, Westminster Abbey (cont.)	8112	d	S	558	
,, ,,	8113	d	S	547	xvi
,, ,,	13154	xi	S	521	
,, ,,	13477	xiv	S	525	
,, ,,	Ch. xxxiii	b	S	928	
,, ,,	Ch. xxxiv	b	S	939	
,, ,,	Ch. xxxv	xxii	S	938	
,, ,,	Ch. xxxvi	?	S	940	
,, ,,	Ch. xxxvii	?	S	937	
,, ,,	Ch. xxxviii	xx	S	935	
,, ,,	Ch. xxxix	xvii	S	936	
Maine-et-Loire, Archives du, Angers	H. 1240	?	H	21	
,, ,,	242 H. 1 (4)	?	S	327	
,, ,,	242 H. 1 (6)	?	H	329	
	Chartes originales du Livre Noir de S. Florent	?	H	799	
Manche, Archives de la, Saint-Lo	destroyed in 1944	?	S	802	
,, ,,	,, ,,	?	M	168	
,, ,,	,, ,,	h	G	443	
,, ,,	,, ,,	?	H	29	
Neufchâtel-en-Bray, Bibliothèque Mun.	,, ,,	?	M	334	
Newcastle upon Tyne, Public Library	Greenwell Deeds D 3	xiii	S	166	
Northamptonshire Record Office, Delapré Abbey, Northampton	Finch-Hatton MS. 170, no. 442 (facs.)	xxi?	S	85	
Nottinghamshire County Records Office, Nottingham	Saville Coll. D.D. S.R. 102/132	xxii	S	739	
Oxford, Bodleian Library	MS. Rawlinson Q. a. 1, f. 26	xiii	S	271	
,, ,,	MS. Charters Essex a. 4. 84	?	S	228	xliii b
,, ,,	MS. Charters Glos. a. 1. 5	xiii	S	351	
,, ,,	MS. Charters Glos. a. 1. 6	xvii	S	346	xx a
,, ,,	MS. Charters Oxon 58	?	S	649	
,, ,,	MS. Charters Salop 107	xxiii	H	379	
,, ,,	Ch. Ch. MSS. Oseney Ch. 878	e	S	626	
,, ,,	Ch. Ch. MSS. Oseney Ch. 879	xiv	M	628	
,, ,,	Ch. Ch. MSS. Oseney Ch. 895	f	M	632	
,, ,,	Ch. Ch. MSS. Oseney Ch. 898	xxii	S	633	
,, ,,	Ch. Ch. MSS. Oseney Ch. 926	f	M	629	
,, ,,	Ch. Ch. MSS. Oseney Ch. 986	e	S	627	
Paris, Archives Nationales	J. 219, no. 1	?	H	438	
,, ,,	K. 23, no. 6⁵	xiii	S	800	viii a
,, ,,	K. 23, no. 15²²	?	G	730	
,, ,,	K. 23, no. 23⁷	xxi	S	801	xxix a
,, ,,	L. 968	?	H	812	
,, ,,	L. 969, no. 379	?	G	808	
,, ,,	L. 969, no. 399	?	G	806	
,, ,,	L. 1018, no. 1²	?	(H)	332	
,, ,,	S. 5057, no. 44	?	M	409	
Paris, Bibliothèque Nationale	Coll. de Bourgogne, vol. 80, no. 32	?	S	444	
,, ,,	Coll. de Bourgogne, vol. 80, no. 247	?	H	206	
	MS. Latin 10083, no. 3	?	M	567	
Rochester Cathedral Muniments (in Kent Archives Office, Maidstone)	B. 780	?	S	718	
Salisbury, Dean and Chapter Muniments (in Salisbury Diocesan Record Office)	C. 2	?	S	271	iii
,, ,,	C. 2	c	S	787	xlviii
,, ,,	C. 2	c	S	788	xlix
,, ,,	C. 3	x	S	786	

Archive or Library	Reference	Scriptor	Grantor	Number in Regesta, vol. iii	Plate in Regesta, vol. iv
Salop Record Office, Shrewsbury	972/14	xxi	S	460	xxxi
Sarthe, Archives de la, Le Mans	H. 1530	?	H	323	
Seine-Maritime, Archives de la, Rouen	7 H. 12	?	GH	304	xxxix
,, ,,	7 H. 12	xxiv	H	305	
,, ,,	8 H. 108	h	G	77	xxxviii
,, ,,	18 H. 1	?	M	909	
,, ,,	20 H. non classé	?	H	731	
,, ,,	untraced	?	G	303	
Stafford, William Salt Library	Marquess of Anglesey MSS. No. 1577	xxiii	H	459	xli
Winchester College Muniments	WCM. 2797	?	M	898	
,, ,,	WCM. 10627	xxiv	H	900	
Worcestershire Record Office, Worcester	Lechmere Coll.	?	S	964	
Private Owners:					
Col. A. Gregory-Hood, Loxley Hall, Warwick		xxi	S	922	xxx
Mrs. Judy Shearn, Red House Farm, Saxmundham, Suffolk (since 1968)		?	S	743	
Mr. Edward Willes, Upper St. Dennis Farm, Honington, Shipston-on-Stour[1]		f?	M	116	xlvii

[1] On 10 July 1968 this charter was bought at Sotheby's by the British Museum, where it is now Add. Ch. 75724.

PLATES

The obverse or majesty side of King Stephen's seals.
(a) and (b) The genuine First Seal (London, The British Museum, Add. Charter 19580 and Seal xxxix. 10). (c) The genuine Second Seal (London, The British Museum, Add. Charter 19581). (d) The forged First Seal (Worcestershire Record Office, Lechmere Collection). The following are the main points of difference between the genuine and the forged First Seal.

GENUINE	FORGED
i. In the legend Є is used.	i. In the legend E is used.
ii. In the legend the final A of GRATIA almost touches the bottom dexter corner (i.e. left as viewed) of the throne.	ii. In the legend the R of REX touches the bottom dexter corner of the throne.
iii. In the legend the point of the sword intervenes between the R and V of ANGLORVM.	iii. In the legend the point of the sword intervenes between the V and M of ANGLORVM.
iv. The dove on the orb is close to the ЄPH of STEPHANVS in the legend.	iv. The dove on the orb is close to the PHA of STEPHANVS in the legend.
v. The supporting columns of the throne have *six* circular ornaments or roundels and are topped by ornaments like pine-cones.	v. The supporting columns of the throne have *eight* roundels and are topped by plain spherical ornaments.
vi. There is a small arch between the king's shin and the column of the throne on either side. Cf. King Harold's throne in the Bayeux Tapestry.	vi. There are no arches between the king's shins and the columns of the throne.
vii. The king's trunk curves in to a narrow waist.	vii. The king's trunk is barrel-like.
viii. The quillons of the sword are short and do not touch the king's sleeve.	viii. The quillons of the sword are long and touch the king's sleeve.
ix. The king's cloak falls from his right shoulder towards his left leg and to the side of the V-shaped folds between the legs.	ix. The king's cloak falls vertically from his right shoulder and directly above the V-shaped folds between the legs.
x. The folds falling from the king's right knee are at angles of about 10°, 45°, 60°, and 72°.	x. The folds falling from the king's right knee form a consistent V-shape at about 72°.
xi. The border of the king's cloak, falling in a V-shape from his shoulders, is ornamented with *six* dots on his left side only.	xi. The border of the king's cloak, falling in a V-shape from his shoulders is ornamented with dots on both sides, the number on his left side being *ten*.

Complete lists of the charters on which these seals are used are given in *Regesta* iii, pp. xv–xvii. For the seal of the Empress see Plate XIII.

PLATE I

a

b

c

d

The reverse or equestrian sides of King Stephen's seals.
(*a*) and (*b*) The genuine First Seal. (*c*) The genuine Second Seal. (*d*) The forged First Seal.
The following are the main points of difference between the genuine and the forged
First Seal.

GENUINE	FORGED
i. In the legend Є is used.	i. In the legend E is used.
ii. The destrier's ears point towards the *left* side of the H in STEPHANVS. and its head is opposite the HA of this word.	ii. The destrier's ears point towards the *right* side of the H in STEPHANVS and its head is opposite the AN of this word.
iii. The destrier's ear almost touches the inner rim of the legend.	iii. There is a wide space between the destrier's head and the inner rim of the legend.
iv. The destrier's fore hooves coincide with the DЄ of DЄI.	iv. The destrier's fore hooves coincide with the EI of DEI.
v. The destrier's tail touches the inner rim of the legend between the final A of GRATIA and the D of DVX.	v. The destrier's tail touches the inner rim of the legend between the D and V of DVX.
vi. The destrier has a flowing mane.	vi. The destrier has a hogged mane.
vii. The king's sword intersects the legend between the third N and O of NORMANNORVM.	vii. The king's sword intersects the legend between the second O and R of NORMANNORVM.
viii. The king's knee is slightly bent and only his toe is in the stirrup.	viii. The king's leg is straight and his instep is in the stirrup.
ix. The king sits erect in the saddle and his sword is nearly vertical. His sword-arm is slightly bent.	ix. The king leans back from the waist and his sword is inclined towards him at an angle of about 80°. His sword-arm is rigidly straight.

See Pl. X for a fragment of a seal, identified by points ii and iii above as the forged First Seal.
Note that in the Second Seal (*c*) the destrier's ears point towards the left side of the H in
STEPHANVS, so this cannot be confused with the forged First Seal.

PLATE II

a

b

c

d

(Salisbury Cathedral, Muniments of the Dean and Chapter, C. 2)

No. **271**

Date: April 1136; at Oxford.

This plate and the two which follow show the surviving examples of Stephen's 'Oxford Charter of Liberties'. Since this was really a charter of liberties for the Church, every bishopric at least would have required an exemplar. The three which survive derive from Salisbury, Exeter, and Hereford. We reproduce them all in order to show how different such exemplars could be in external appearance. The scribe of this version which derives from Salisbury has not been identified, but even a private scribe of the Bishop of Salisbury would probably have had contacts with the royal Scriptorium in the period when Bishop Roger was the justiciar and his son the chancellor.

The wording of the dating clause corresponds with the Exeter, not with the Hereford, version. The main clauses of this text, unlike the other two, are distinguished by wedge-shaped paragraph-marks. There is no sign of a lacuna having been filled in (lines 12–15) as in the Hereford version (q.v.). The handwriting is slightly compressed in parts, e.g. line 11, but this does not seem to have any significance. Though not identical, it has a strong family-resemblance to that of Plates xlviii–l.

PLATE III

Ego Steph's dei gra assensu cleri z populi in rege anglie electus z a Will'o Cantuar' archiep'o z Sce Romane eccle legato consecratus z ab Innocentio sce Romane sedis pontifice p'modu confirmat' respectu z amore dei scam ecclam libera esse concedo z debita reuerentia illi confirmo. Nichil in ea in reb eccliasticis simoniace detur uel emat'. Omes itaq p'sonas z oīa q̄ ad eas p'tinent cum dignitate z libertate sua eisdem custodienda z confirmanda concedo. ... Omes ecclasticas p'sonas z oes clicos z res eorum in manu z custodia z iusticia mea suscipio. ...

Dat' ... apud Oxenef'. Anno ab incarnac'oe d'ni M°C°xxx°vi°.

(Exeter Cathedral Dean and Chapter MS. 2529)

No. **271**

Date: April 1136, at Oxford.

This plate shows the Exeter version of the 'Oxford Charter of Liberties', written by an unidentified scribe. The cords and unidentifiable fragment of a seal have been wrongly and very clumsily attached (perhaps by Dean Lyttelton) to this charter, the bottom left-hand corner of which may be the residual stub of a tongue for the seal. There is no sign of a space having been filled in at the point in this text (lines 9 and 10) corresponding with the seeming insertion in the Hereford version (Pl. V).

PLATE IV

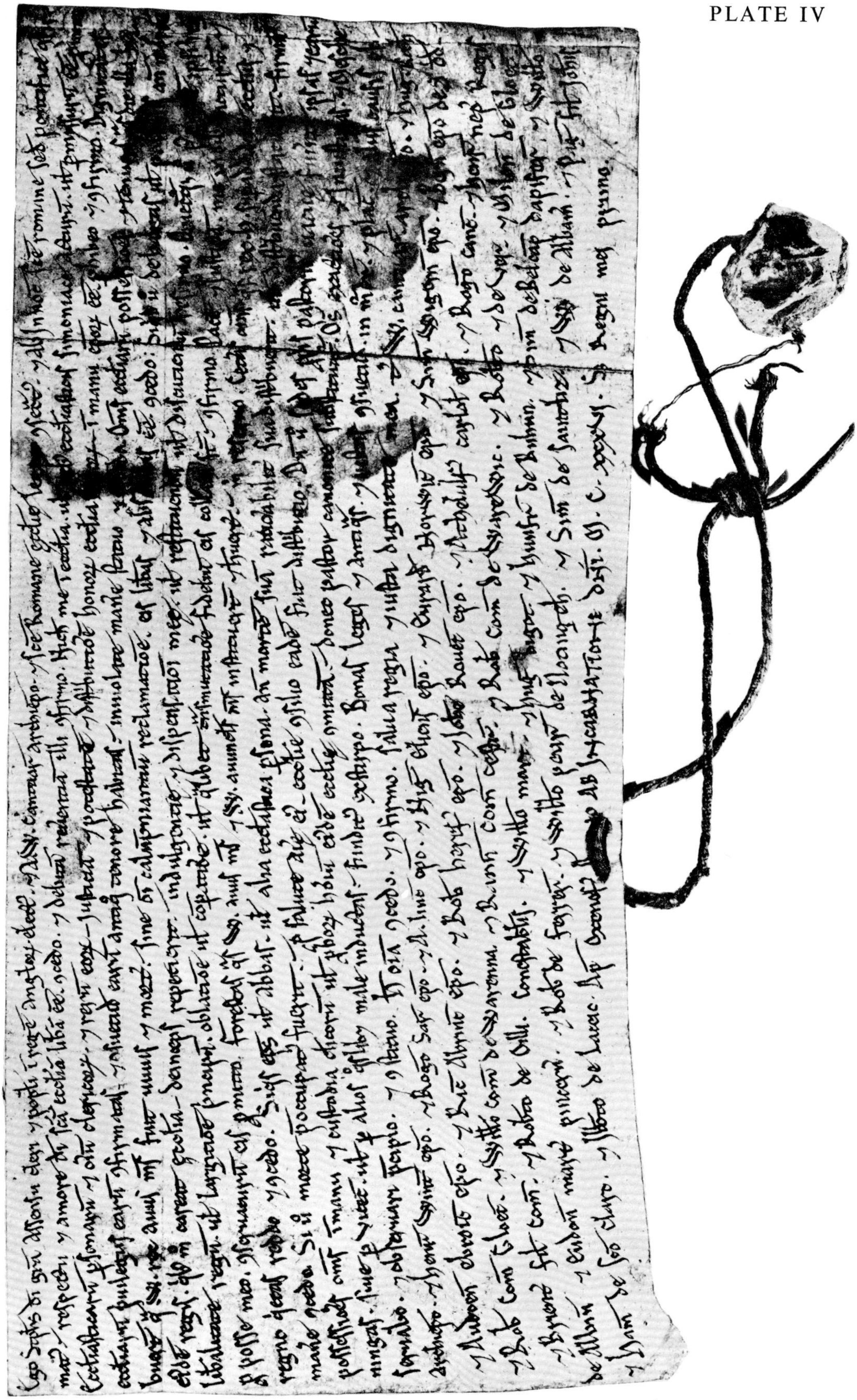

(Oxford, Bodleian Library MS. Rawlinson, Q. a. 1. f. 26)

No. **271**

Date: April 1136, at Oxford.

This version, which derives from Hereford, is in a scrapbook collected by Thomas Hearne and is endorsed *De libertate Her(efordensis) ecclesie*. It has a tongue and the stub of a wrapper but no seal has survived. The hand is that of Scriptor XIII and Mr. Bishop has suggested that this was a late draft, which was eventually sealed and issued, because so many 'originals' had to be sent out.[1] The reason for this suggestion is obvious from a glance at the document. It looks as if a space had been left between *concedo*, near the end of line 15 and *et ipse*, near the end of line 18, to be filled later, perhaps, by a form of words not yet agreed. The space left seems to have been inadequate for the matter to be inserted and the scribe seems to have had to use a smaller, more compressed hand. It is not, however, clear to us that the words inserted in this space correspond precisely with a complete clause of the charter. To do so, the insertion should end at *distributio* in line 18 or else at *canonice substituatur* in line 20 (where, in fact, a paragraph mark occurs in the Salisbury version). It would indeed be interesting if the disposal of the property of deceased clerics had caused difficulty in the final negotiation of this agreement between Stephen and the Church and had been clearly reflected in a draft version. It seems to us more likely that the explanation of the compressed passage is a physical one. The scribe may have been writing on a narrow desk or ledge and perhaps he tried to squeeze in an extra line before rearranging his parchment. There was a good deal still to write and he may have feared that without compression his parchment would not be big enough.

The peculiar diplomatic structure of this document is due to the fact that it records an agreement, which made it difficult to follow the normal diplomatic sequence. The superscription is unique and certainly not a mere scribal invention. The dating clause differs from that used in the Exeter and Salisbury versions, which read *sed regni mei primo* instead of *in communi concilio*.

[1] T. A. M. Bishop, *Scriptores Regis*, 34 and pl. v.

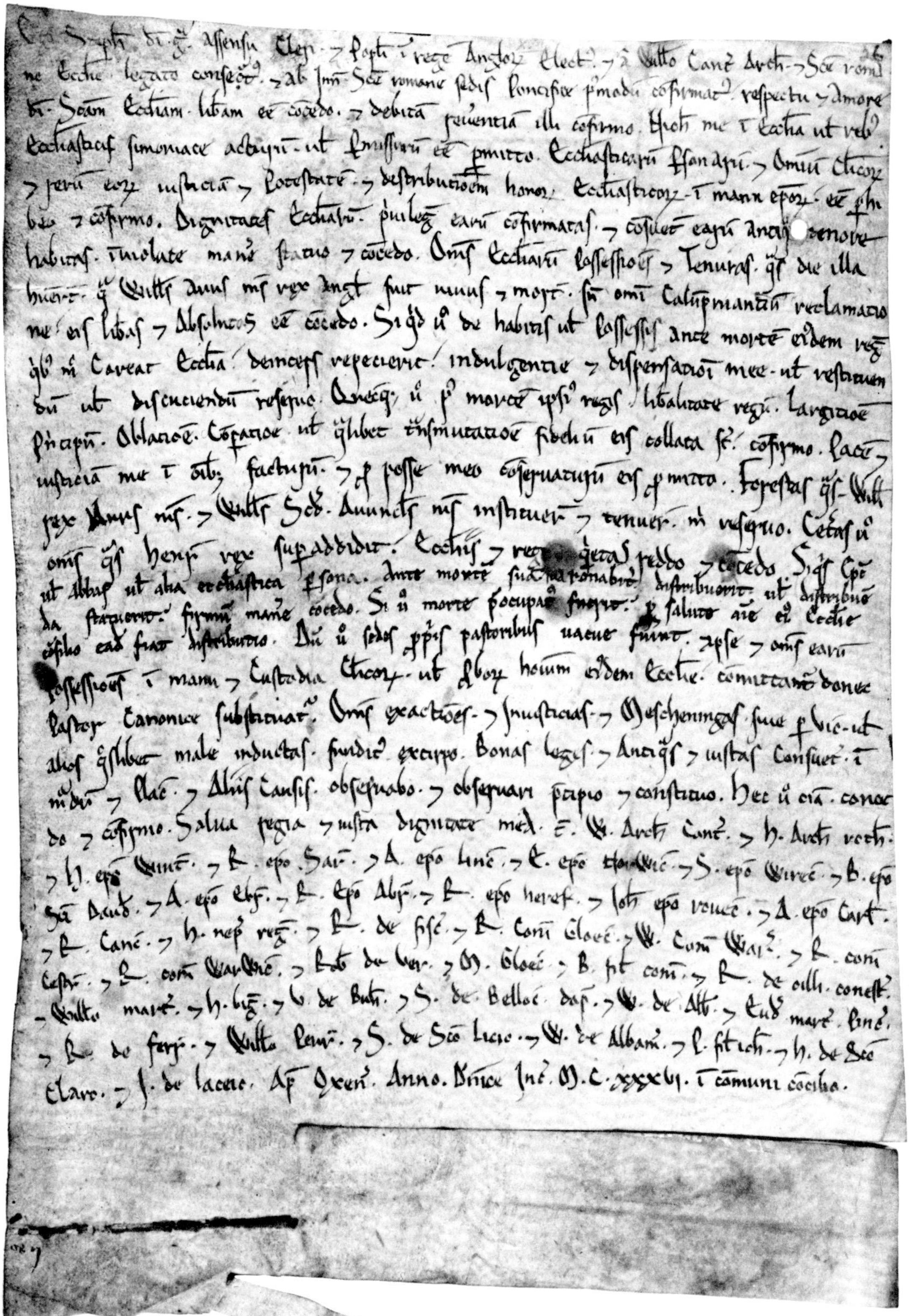

Ego Stephanus Dei gratia assensu cleri et populi in regem Anglorum electus, et a Willelmo Cantuariensi archiepiscopo et sancte Romane ecclesie legato consecratus, et ab Innocentio sancte Romane sedis pontifice postmodum confirmatus, respectu et amore Dei sanctam ecclesiam liberam esse concedo, et debitam reverentiam illi confirmo. Nichil me in ecclesia vel rebus ecclesiasticis simoniace acturum vel permissurum esse promitto. Ecclesiasticarum personarum et omnium clericorum et rerum eorum iusticiam et potestatem et distributionem honorum ecclesiasticorum in manu episcoporum esse perhibeo et confirmo. Dignitates ecclesiarum privilegiis earum confirmatas et consuetudines earum antiquo tenore habitas inviolate manere statuo et concedo. Omnes ecclesiarum possessiones et tenuras quas die illa habuerunt qua Willelmus rex avus meus fuit vivus et mortuus, sine omni calumpniantium reclamatione eis liberas et absolutas esse concedo. Si quid vero de habitis vel possessis ante mortem eiusdem regis quibus modo careat ecclesia deinceps repetierit, indulgentie et dispensationi mee vel restituendum vel discutiendum reservo. Quecunque vero post mortem ipsius regis liberalitate regum, largitione principum, oblatione, comparatione, vel qualibet transmutatione fidelium eis collata sunt, confirmo. Pacem et iusticiam me in omnibus facturum et pro posse meo conservaturum eis promitto. Forestas quas Willelmus rex avus meus et Willelmus secundus avunculus meus instituerunt et tenuerunt mihi reservo. Ceteras vero omnes quas Henricus rex superaddidit ecclesiis et regno quietas reddo et concedo. Si quis episcopus vel abbas vel alia ecclesiastica persona ante mortem suam rationabiliter sua distribuerit vel distribuenda statuerit, firmum manere concedo. Si vero morte preoccupatus fuerit, pro salute anime eius ecclesie consilio eadem fiat distributio. Dum vero sedes propriis pastoribus vacue fuerint, ipse et omnes earum possessiones in manu et custodia clericorum vel proborum hominum eiusdem ecclesie committantur donec pastor canonice substituatur. Omnes exactiones et iniusticias et meschenningas sive per vicecomites vel per alios quoslibet male inductas funditus extirpo. Bonas leges et antiquas et iustas consuetudines in murdris et placitis et aliis causis observabo et observari precipio et constituo. Hec vero omnia concedo et confirmo, salva regia et iusta dignitate mea. T. W. Archi Cant. et H. Archi Rothom. et H. epo Wint. et R. epo Sar. et A. epo Linc. et E. epo Norwic. et S. epo Wirec. et B. epo Sci David. et A. epo Ebr. et R. epo Abr. et R. epo Heref. et Ioh. epo Rovec. et A. epo Cart. et R. Canc. et H. nep. reg. et R. de Fisc. et R. Com. Gloec. et W. Com. Warr. et R. com. Cestr. et R. com. Warwic. et Rob. de Ver. et M. Gloec. et B. fil. com. et R. de Oilli conest. et Willo Mart. et H. Big. et H. de Buh. et S. de Belloc dap. et W. de Alb. et Eud. Mart. pinc. et R. de Ferr. et Willo Peur. et S. de Sco Lecio et W. de Albam. et P. fil. Ioh. et H. de Sco Claro et I. de Lacei. Ap. Oxen. Anno Dnice Inc. M.C.XXXVI. in comuni concilio.

cms

(Beverley Corporation Records, No. 2, Schedule 1)

No. **99**

Date: Feb. 1136, at York.

King Stephen confirms to Beverley Minster its banleuca and other rights, including its five days' fair and its thraves in the East Riding.

There is a fragment of Stephen's first seal in white wax on a tag passed through two slits in the bottom fold. This charter is in the hand of Scriptor XIII. He wrote 21 of the surviving original charters and writs of Henry I, 12 of Stephen, and one for Robert de Sigillo, Bishop of London, who was formerly head of the Scriptorium and *Custos Sigilli* (as his name indicates) under Henry I. His hand is also found in a charter for Reading Abbey (Pl. VIII *b*) which bears an unmistakable fragment of the forged First Seal of Stephen. Scriptor XIII writes a firm but sometimes rather blotchy and unattractive hand—Mr. Bishop has called it 'awkward and insensitive'. His composi-tions are often formulated so elaborately and pretentiously that they would be suspect if we knew them only in transcripts and not in an identifiable hand employed in many royal charters of two reigns. He could also, on occasion, draft an admirably concise charter or writ and some of his less inflated products confront us with the gravest difficulties. His work is, not infrequently, marred by careless draftsmanship, and mistakes in dating (to which he is especially prone), spelling, and ab-breviation.

The present charter is not an extreme example of Scriptor XIII's inflated formulation, but is more elaborately worded than most royal scribes would have made it, and several of his charac-teristic tricks of style may be observed. The 'general' address is oddly truncated, earls, justices, barons, and *ministri* being omitted. The opening of the dispositive clause (line 2) is not in the form customarily used by royal scribes. The word-order and rhythm of the ensuing sentences is charac-teristic of this scribe and so, especially, is the wording of the confirmation at the end of the injunc-tive clause (line 16). A clause of this type was sometimes used by other royal scribes, but Scriptor XIII uses it with great frequency. The charter is dated both by the year of the Incarnation (in the style, necessarily, of Lady Day after Christmas) and by the regnal year (cf. Pl. IX).

PLATE VI

(Belvoir Castle, MSS. of the Duke of Rutland, Royal Grants no. 479)

No. **716**

Date: Feb.–March 1136, at York.

King Stephen confirms Walter Espec's foundation Charter for Rievaulx Abbey, and he acquits the land of 'tenmantale', Danegeld, and all aids and secular service.

The text of the Charter printed in *Regesta* iii, **716**, has been conjecturally restored with the aid of Henry I's Charter (*Regesta* ii, **1782**). This document is written in the hand of Scriptor XIII. The seal, which is attached to a bottom fold by a parchment tag, is a good impression of Stephen's (genuine) First Seal in white wax now stained red. The witnesses are described in an unusual phrase, which is only partly legible in this manuscript, [*Testibus subscriptis in quorum audientia* etc. *hec* . . .] *mee concessa sunt*. The calendar date, following the place-date, is written in full, not in Roman figures, and the regnal year is also given. This is followed by *in* and quite possibly the following words were *communi concilio*. We are inclined to say that this charter was not exactly a run-of-the-mill product of the royal Scriptorium, but a distinctive product of this scribe.

PLATE VII

a (Paris, Archives Nationales K. 23. 6⁵)

No. **800**

Date: probably 1136, at Gillingham.

King Stephen notifies William (Warelwast) Bishop of Exeter, that he has granted to the Abbot of Savigny the church of Buckfastleigh with its lands etc. for the establishment there of an abbey of the Order of Savigny, and he requests the bishop to give him seisin of the things that pertain to him.

We believe this is written in the hand of Scriptor XIII. It is a brief and clear command to the bishop, and the wording of the injunctive clause (in lines 3 and 4) is of considerable interest. The word *precipio* is avoided, and it reads *mando tibi et volo ut de his que tibi pertinent eum benigne saisias*. There is a 'movent' in the form *quia hoc facio pro servitio dei* etc. The high rank of the two ecclesiastical witnesses is also worthy of comment. It would seem that at this time Stephen had a very tender care for the susceptibilities of the Church and the episcopate.

b (London, The British Museum, Add. Charter 19580)

No. **688**

Date: 1135–9, at Westminster.

King Stephen orders that the Abbot of Reading hold his land at Rowington (Warwickshire) with quittances as in the time of Henry I.

This writ (*precipio*) in the hand of Scriptor XIII bears an impression of the genuine First Seal of Stephen in white wax on a tongue partially torn and repaired by sewing. It is addressed for Warwickshire, and the earl, who is sometimes omitted from the address of such writs, takes his rightful formal place after the bishop. The concluding sentence beginning *Quia ecclesia illa in manu et tutela m[ea est]* looks almost like an afterthought, but it might properly have formed part of a dispositive clause which is missing from this writ.

PLATE VIII

a

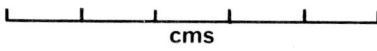

b

cms

(London, The British Museum, MS. Cotton Nero C. III. f. 177)

No. **132**

Date: August 1138, at the siege of Shrewsbury.

King Stephen confirms to Buildwas Abbey the manor of Buildwas (Salop), given by Roger, Bishop of Chester, which was rated at one hide. He frees it from scot and lot, geld and Danegeld, aids, castle-work, bridge-work, army duty, and all secular service.

No trace remains of a tongue or other means of appending the seal. Written in the hand of Scriptor XIII, this charter is given rather an ecclesiastical appearance by the elongated capitals in the first line.[1] The calendar and regnal years are placed after, not before, the place-date. The regnal year corresponds with the siege of Shrewsbury in August, 1138. The calendar year can correspond only if the scribe has used the logical but un-English style of beginning the year on Lady Day *before* Christmas. In the Beverley Charter (Pl. VI) calendar and regnal years correspond on the assumption that he uses the English Style of beginning the year on Lady Day *after* Christmas. Scriptor XIII seems to be both inconsistent and inaccurate in his dating. The witnesses of this charter are not incompatible with the place-date, but it is disconcerting to find that the charter recording Bishop Roger's gift to Buildwas does not seem to have been issued till 1145 or 1146.[2] It is not, however, impossible that the formal gift was made orally *coram rege* (line 4) seven or eight years earlier and it would have been prudent of the monks of Buildwas to obtain a royal confirmation without delay. The draftsmanship of this charter is, for Scriptor XIII, restrained, but some of his stylistic traits are obvious: e.g. *amodo usque in sempiternum* (line 8), a favourite phrase, and *subsequentium attestatione communio* (line 10) instead of the normal *Hiis testibus*. The emphatic *quietum dico et liberum* (line 6) is not uncommon, for scribes seem sometimes to reproduce faithfully in writing an original oral emphasis.

[1] Cf. Pl. XI, the charter written by Scriptor XIII for Robert de Sigillo, Bishop of London.
[2] R. W. Eyton, *Antiquities of Shropshire*, vi, 323.

PLATE IX

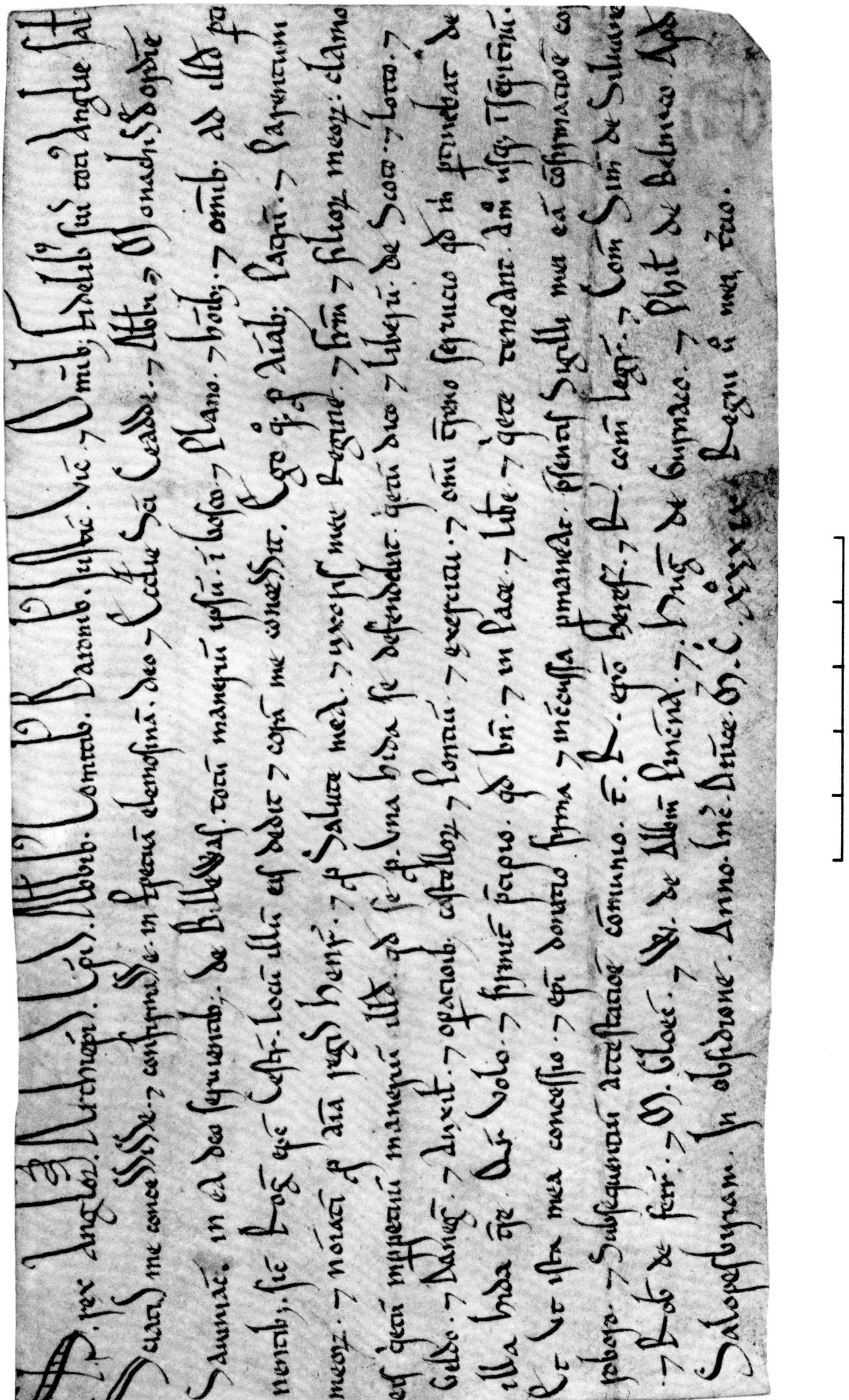

(Hertford County Record Office, AS. 1)

No. **679**

Date: Ostensibly Dec. 1138–June 1139, at Arundel (if it were genuine).

This pretended original purports to be a confirmation by Stephen to Reading Abbey of the manor, church etc. of Aston (Herts.) and 100 solidates in Stanton Harcourt (Oxon.) given by Queen Adeliza (widow of Henry I).

This charter, written in the hand of Scriptor XIII, is of quite exceptional interest for, although it is written by a well-known and prolific royal scribe, it bears upon the tongue (which has been very nearly, but not quite, torn off and stitched on again) a small fragment of a seal which, from the position of the destrier's head in relation to the legend and its inner rim, is undoubtedly the forged First Seal of Stephen.[1] In diplomatic form this confirmation is very ordinary and contains none of Scriptor XIII's more elaborate clauses, though he does use (line 7) *amodo usque in sempiternum*, a phrase which flows naturally from his pen. Apart even from the seal fragment, this charter gives rise to suspicion. Queen Adeliza held Aston as part of her dower and ought not to have alienated it. The regularizing of this gift may have been the object of this forged confirmation. Further, at such an ostensible date it is surprising to find no indication that William d'Aubigny *pincerna* (line 9) was either an earl or married to Queen Adeliza. The charter, if genuine, could not have been issued earlier than December, 1138, because Robert de Ferrers (line 8) was created an earl in August of that year[2] and Waleran, Count of Meulan (line 8) was in Normandy from May 1138 till December 1139. The lower limit of date is given by the (pretended) First Seal, which should not have been in use after the dismissal of Roger the Chancellor in June, 1139. It may be that Abbot Reginald (1151–4/8), who was deposed, was involved in this forgery by a royal scribe, since he is said to have acted on some occasions as Stephen's deputy Chancellor.[3] The scribe may have acted innocently.

[1] Cf. Pl. II.
[2] Robert de Ferrers is described (as here) as Earl of Nottingham instead of Derby in only one other royal charter (**308**).
[3] See *Regesta* iii, xi.

PLATE X

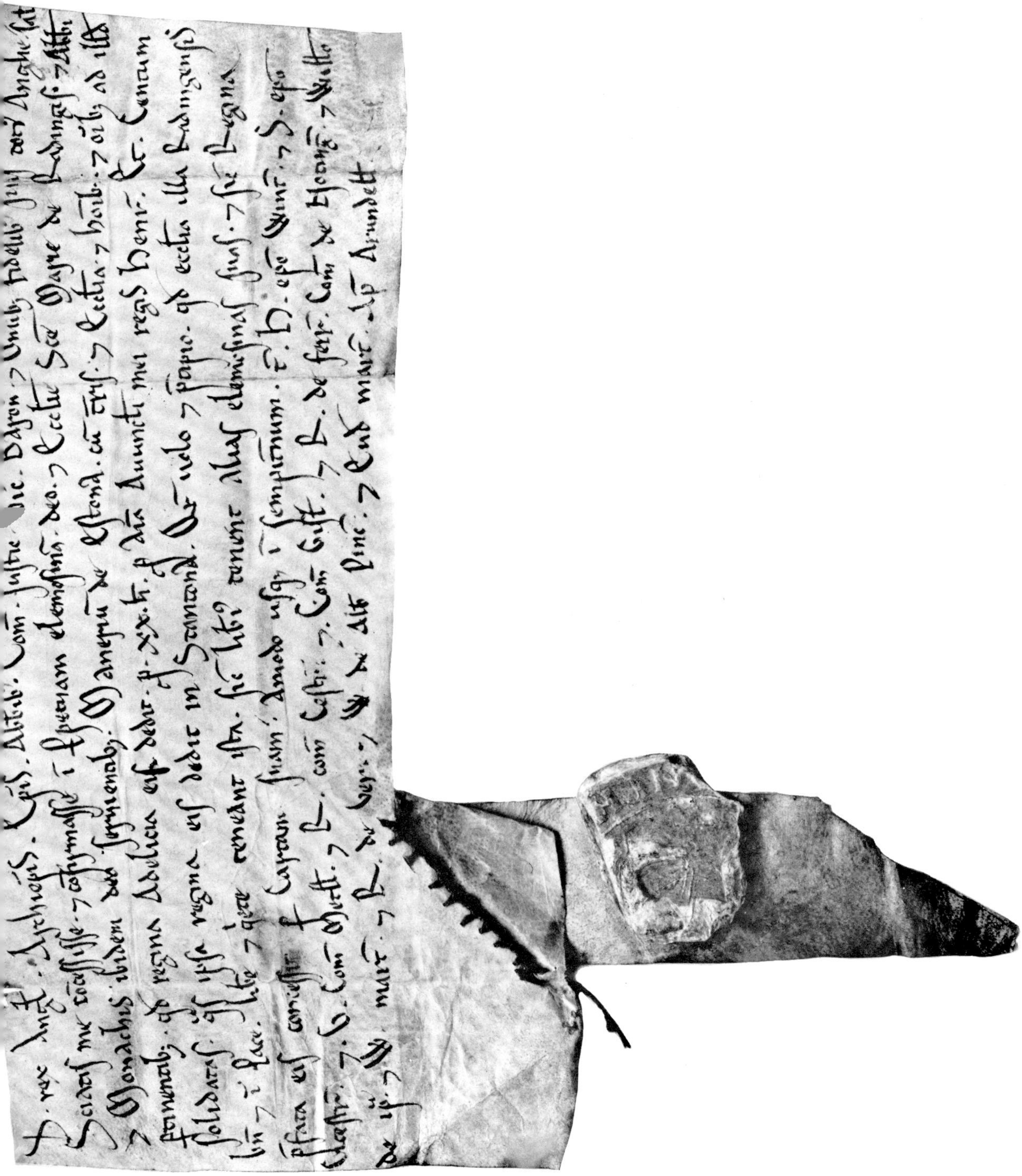

(London, Muniments of the Dean and Chapter of St. Paul's, A40/1443)

This episcopal charter is not included in *Regesta* iii.

Date: Easter, 1142, at London.

Robert de Sigillo, Bishop of London, notifies the Dean, Archdeacon, Chapter, and barons of St. Paul's that since Ranulf Peverel had given Abberton (Essex) for the lighting of St. Paul's, by the hand of the Dean and Chapter, he restores and confirms the land to the Dean and Chapter for that purpose.

This charter is in the hand of Scriptor XIII, which suggests that he was employed by the Bishop of London, his former superior in the royal Scriptorium, after he left the royal service. The text was published by Miss Marion Gibbs in *Early Charters of the Cathedral Church of St. Paul, London* (Camden Third Ser. lviii, 1939) No. 219. The scribe has obviously fallen very easily into the appropriate episcopal style. The words *Et ut hec confirmatio nostra . . . presenti Sigilli nostri impressione munimus* (lines 10–11) echo a formula he often used in royal charters. This charter is dated both by the year of the Incarnation and by the episcopal year, preceding the list of witnesses, which is followed by the place-date and the reference to Easter. The dates in this case (about which Scriptor XIII was notoriously careless) are consistent with each other and with all the other available evidence.

We have reproduced this charter for comparison with some of those which Scriptor XIII wrote in the royal service; a comparison from which it emerges with credit. Both in external appearance and in draftsmanship it is a dignified and appropriate episcopal charter. It is not clear how the seal was appended.

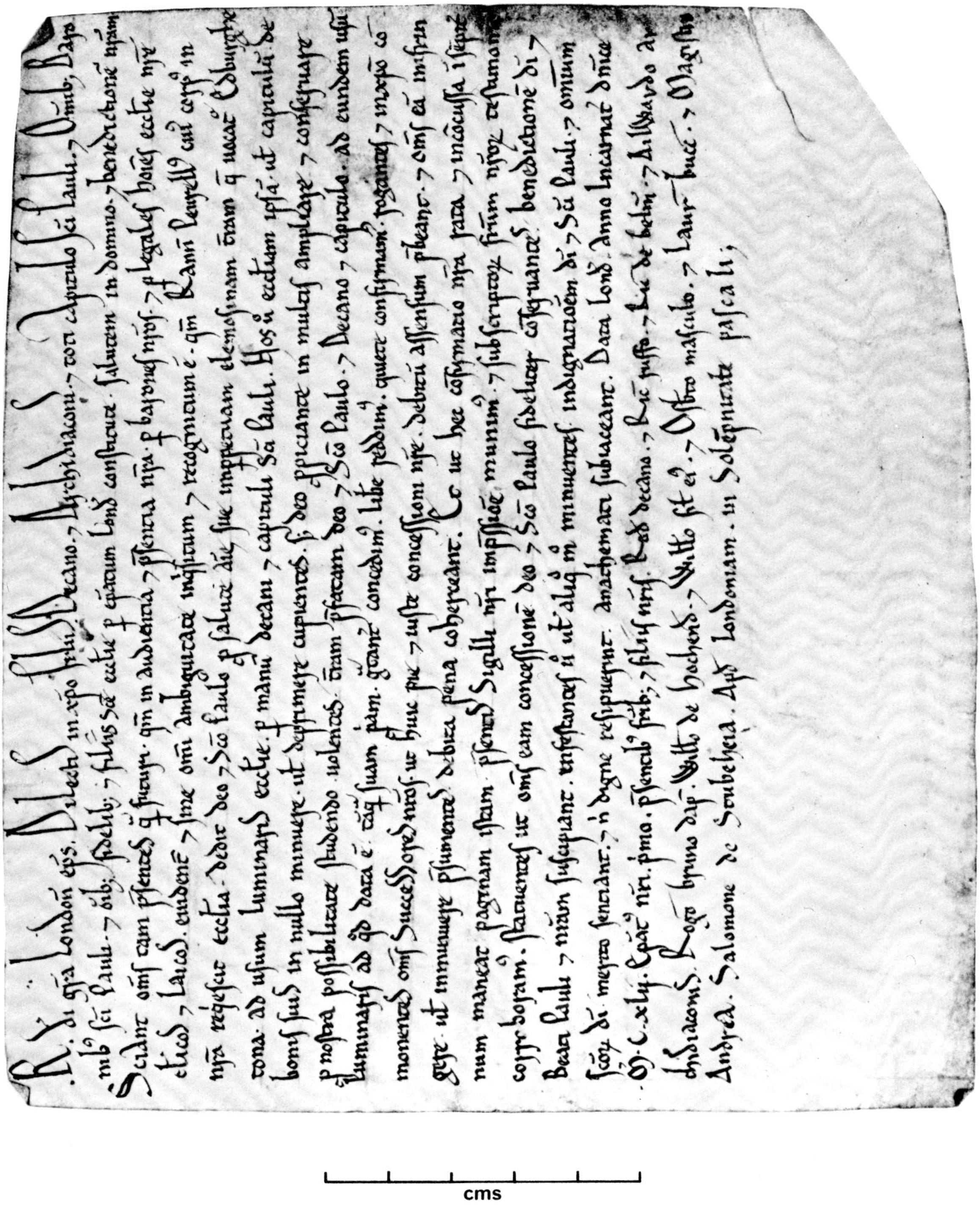

.R. di gra London' eps. Dilectis in xpo filiis Decano. 7 Archidiacono. 7 toti capitulo sci Pauli. 7 Omib; Baronib; sci Pauli. 7 oib; fidelib; 7 filiis sce ecclie p episcopatum Lond constitute. salutem in domino. 7 benedictione nram.
Sciant omis tam psentes q futuri. qm in audientia 7 psentia nra. p barones nros. 7 p legales hoies ecclie nre
clericos 7 laicos. euidenter 7 sine omi ambiguitate inquisitum 7 recognitum e. qm Rann Peurell cui corpus in
nra requiescit ecclia. dedit deo 7 sco Paulo p salute aie sue in ppetuam elemosinam terram q uocat Edburghe-
tona. ad usum luminaris ecclie. p manu decani 7 capituli sci Pauli. Nos u ecclesiam ipsa ut capitulum de
bonis suis in nullo minuere ut deprimere cupientes. s; deo ppiciante in multis ampliare 7 conseruare
p nostra possibilitate studendo uolentes. terram pfatam deo 7 sco Paulo. 7 Decano 7 capitulo. ad eundem usu
luminaris ad qd data e. tanq suam ppriam. grant concedim. libe reddim. quiete confirmam. rogantes 7 in xpo co-
monentes omis Successores nros. ut huic pie 7 iuste concessioni nre. debitu assensum pbeant. 7 omis ea infrin-
gere ut imminuere psumentes debita pena coherceant. Et ut hec confirmatio nra rata 7 inconcussa i sempiternum maneat paginam istam psentis Sigilli nri impssione munim. 7 subscriptorum frium nrorum testimonio
corroboram. statuentes ut omis eam concessione deo 7 sco Paulo fideliter conseruantes benedictione di 7
Beati Pauli 7 nram suscipiant. infestantes u ut aliq modo minuentes indignationem di 7 sci Pauli 7 omium
scorum di inperpetuo sentiant. 7 ni digne resipuerint. anathemati subiaceant. Data Lond. anno Incarnat dnice
M.C.xlii. Epat nri. pmo. psentib; frib; 7 filiis nris. Rad decano. 7 Ric ruffo. 7 Ric de belm. 7 Ailwardo ar-
chidiaconis. Rogo bruno dap. Willo de hochend. 7 Willo fit ei. 7 Osbto masculo. 7 Laur buce. 7 Magistro
Andrea. Salomone de Stubeheia. Apd Londoniam. in Solepnitate pascali;

a (Ely Cathedral, Muniments of the Dean and Chapter, Charter 8 B)

No. **260**

Date: 1136–40, at Reading.

King Stephen orders the Reeve of Dunwich to restore, without delay, to the monks of Ely the herring owed them by the men of Dunwich, by way of custom, and to do the monks full justice, both in this matter and concerning the transport.

This writ is in the hand of Scriptor XIV, whom Mr. Bishop identified as Peter the Scribe.[1] He had a long career in the service of Henry I, Stephen, the Empress, and Theobald, Archbishop of Canterbury. His hand is also found in a letter of Nigel, Bishop of Ely and in a Charter of the Prior of Christ Church, Canterbury, in favour of Peter the Scribe himself. It seeems probable that he entered the service of the Empress after the Battle of Lincoln. We have already indicated the apparent gap in Scriptor XIV's career between the early part of 1144, when he was working for the Empress, and 1146 or 1147 when he was employed by Archbishop Theobald.[2] We have also hazarded the opinion that he, himself, and not, as Mr. Bishop suggested, an imitator,[3] wrote a series of charters for St. Martin le Grand, London,[4] and we think it possible that he was a resident canon there, or at least a scribal employee, after he left the service of the Empress and before he entered that of the archbishop.

The present writ begins, not with a *Precipio*, but with a simple, direct imperative, somewhat rare at this date. It seems comparable with later Writs of Debt and Entry. Concise in the extreme, no unnecessary phrase or word is used. As usual in writs of this kind, there is only one witness. The name Vere is commonly written, as here, with a V and an *er* abbreviation-sign.

[1] *Scriptores Regis*, 24–5 and pl. xvii b.
[2] *Regesta* iii, p. xiv.
[3] *Scriptores Regis*, 8.
[4] *Regesta* iii, p. xv and nos. **540, 545, 547, 549, 552, 558, 559.**

b (London, The Public Record Office, D.L. 10/11)

No. **388**

Date: 1135–9; place-date missing.

King Stephen grants to Miles (?) of Gloucester and his heirs, in fee (the custody of Gloucester castle and the shrievalty (of Gloucestershire?) and other tenures etc.).

This fragment of a charter, addressed generally for England and Wales, is written in the hand of Scriptor XIV, and bears on a tongue a damaged impression of Stephen's (genuine) First Seal in white wax. Since certain phrases, such as *sicut rex et d* . . . (in line 8), seem to correspond exactly with phrases used in Nos. **386** and **387** in favour of Miles of Gloucester, there is a temptation, in the absence of a transcript, to fill in some of the lacunae from these sources. It must be resisted because it could only result in guesswork, not a definitely established text, even though it seems clear, from what remains, that it is concerned with matters that are mentioned in the other grants. The only witness whose name remains in full is an unusual one in Stephen's charters (Elyas Giffard) who does, however, witness the charter of the Empress creating Miles Earl of Hereford.

PLATE XII

a

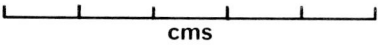

b

(London, the Public Record Office, D.L. 10/17)

No. **394**

Date: 25 July 1141–Dec. 1142, at Oxford.

The Empress grants to Miles of Gloucester, Earl of Hereford, and his heirs the castle and honour of Abergavenny to be held hereditarily in fee from Brian fitzCount and his wife, Matilda, and their heirs for the service of three knights.

This charter bears the seal of the Empress in white wax on a tongue. It appears to be written in the hand of Scriptor XIV. The superscription is that customarily used by the Empress as *Anglorum Domina* and it is addressed generally for England and Wales in the usual regal form. The text of the charter consists of a dispositive clause only. It begins with a somewhat unusual, because wholly secular, 'movent' which shows that, in effect, the Empress was simply confirming an agreement between the beneficiary and Brian and Matilda of Wallingford. Cf. Pl. XXVII *a*.

The seal of the Empress is smaller than an ordinary royal seal and has an obverse or majesty side only. It bears the legend +MATHILDIS DEI GRATIA ROMANORVM REGINA and was clearly made for her in Germany or Italy during the lifetime of her first husband, the Emperor Henry V (d. 1125). It is strange that the Empress continued to use this seal even after she became Countess of Anjou and Lady of the English. Presumably she considered that her imperial title overrode all others, though in that case it is also curious that she continued to use a seal which denied her the title of Empress and styled her only Queen of the Romans, probably because she had not been crowned in Rome. Cf. Pl. XV.

PLATE XIII

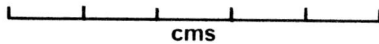

cms

(London, The British Museum, Cotton Charter XVI. 27)

No. **274**

Date: Midsummer, 1141, at Westminster.

The first charter of the Empress for Geoffrey de Mandeville, Earl of Essex (damaged in the Cottonian fire).

The charter seems to have had a bottom fold to take a tag or cords for the seal. Written in the hand of Scriptor XIV, it is reproduced here because of its intrinsic interest, for it was upon these terms, amplified in the second charter of the Empress, 25–31 July, 1141 (No. **275**) that Geoffrey de Mandeville entered Maud's allegiance. This is an elaborate document, much more in the nature of an agreement than a royal charter normally was. The superscription of the Empress is, for this date, incorrect. As though to remedy this defect, the scribe gives her correct, formal title in the dispositive clause, virtually beginning afresh: *Sciant omnes tam presentes quam futuri quod ego Matildis regis Henrici filia et Anglorum domina do et concedo* (if the later transcripts are to be trusted). This more resembles the wording of a private than of a royal charter. The dispositive clause contains, necessarily in the circumstances, more conditional clauses than usual. Certain phrases, such as *Et ut sit capitalis justicia in Essexa hereditabiliter mea et heredum meorum*, strongly emphasize the hereditary nature of the tenures. These features produce an unusual and complex dispositive clause. In contrast, the injunctive clause is very concise but unusual in form. It begins, not with the customary *Quare volo* etc., but: *Et ei firmiter concedo et heredibus suis quod bene in pace et libere et sine placito habeat et teneat hereditabiliter, sicut hec carta confirmat* etc. Indeed the whole clause, with its *quamdiu se defendere potuerit de scelere sive traditione ad corpus meum pertinente per se aut per unum militem si quis coram venerit qui eum appellare voluerit*, is as uncommon a piece of Latinity as of diplomatic construction. It is instinct with the spirit of the feudal aristocracy and an atmosphere of mutual trust is obviously lacking. A somewhat disconcerted Scriptor XIV, one feels, did his best in unusual and difficult circumstances. and produced something more resembling a private than a royal charter.

PLATE XIV

cms

(Cambridge, King's College Muniments, 2.W.1)

No. **651**

Date: July 1141–December 1142, at Oxford.

The Empress confirms the chapel of St. James at Exeter to the Abbey of Saint Martin des Champs, Paris.

Written, we believe, in the hand of Scriptor XIV, with a good impression of Maud's seal in white wax on a tongue doubled lengthwise.

The draftsmanship, apart from the hand, suggests a scribe who had experience in the royal Scriptorium. The superscription, general address for England, dispositive and injunctive clauses are correct and concise. The upper and lower limits of date are given by Miles of Gloucester's creation as Earl of Hereford, and by Maud's escape from Oxford.

For comment on the seal of the Empress see notes to Pl. XIII.

It should be pointed out that, for photographic purposes, manuscript and seal generally require different lighting and it is difficult, if not impossible, to obtain entirely satisfactory photographs of both in the same exposure. In this, as in several other cases, we have preferred a clear text to a more sharply defined seal.

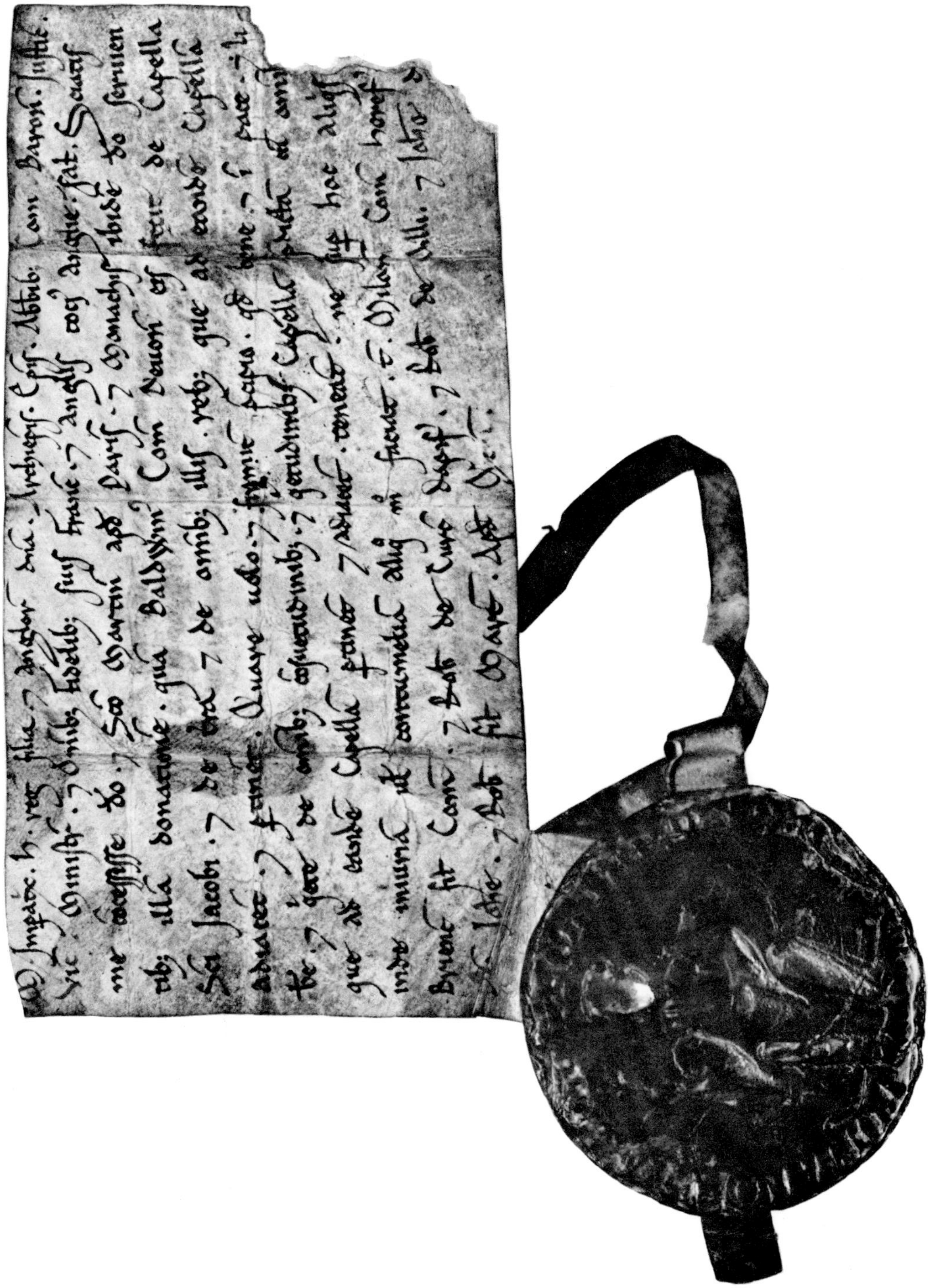

PLATE XV

(London, Westminster Abbey Muniments, 8113)

No. **547**

Date: 1147–52, at London.

King Stephen orders Richard de Lucy the justice and Maurice the sheriff of Essex to reseise Henry, Bishop of Winchester, and the canons of St. Martin le Grand of their marsh at Maldon (Essex), given to the church of St. Mary, Maldon, by Rannulf de Venions, as it was recognized and sworn in the hundred court of Maldon before sheriff Maurice that they had it in the time of Henry I and afterwards till Walter fitzGilbert set out for Jerusalem. They are not to be unjustly (*sic*) impleaded till he returns.

This writ (*precipio*) is, we believe, in the hand of Scriptor XIV, though Mr. Bishop thinks that it was written by an imitator (**d**). It bears a much worn impression of Stephen's Second Seal in white wax and we take it to be genuine. This is an argument in favour of the authenticity of the other St. Martin's writs in the same hand.[1] This is a matter of some interest because a number of these seem to approximate more nearly than other originals of this date to the forms of writs in Glanvill. The present writ seems to be a writ for execution of judgment following a case of disseisin settled by a hundredal jury of recognition. Perhaps this was not regarded as a final settlement since (lines 7 and 8) the canons are not to be impleaded unjustly—an unfortunate phrase—till Walter fitzGilbert returns from Jerusalem. The writ also requires (lines 9 and 10) that justice be done to the canons in respect of injuries. Finally, instead of *ne inde audiam clamorem* etc., the scribe has written *ita ne rectum meum obliviscatur si ibi fuerit*, a significant phrase which we do not remember having seen in any other contemporary writ. Unusual phrases do indeed occur in several St. Martin's documents. So, in **548**, Queen Matilda, at the end of a writ and perhaps of her patience, says: *Sentiant itaque prescripti canonici ipsis apud nos profuisse quod ego pro eis rogo.*

[1] **540, 545, 549, 552, 558, 559.**

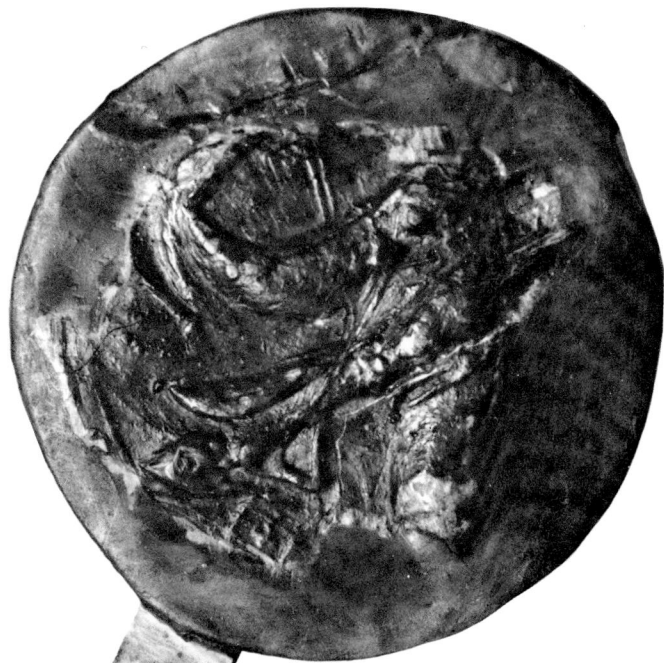

PLATE XVI

(London, Westminster Abbey Muniments, 8110)

No. **549**

Date: 1143–54, at Bermondsey.

King Stephen directs Richard de Lucy the justice and the sheriff of Essex that the Bishop of Winchester (Dean of St. Martin le Grand) and the canons are to have their marsh at Maldon (Essex).

Written, in our opinion, in the hand of Scriptor XIV (though Mr. Bishop attributes it to his imitator (**d**)), this writ (*precipio*) may be called a Writ of Right since the words *Et si quis illis fecerit iniuriam precipio quod plenum rectum illis faciatis inde* are used. It differs from the classical Glanvill writ in that both justice and sheriff are addressed, but perhaps the effect was much the same. We think that Richard de Lucy is probably addressed here as justice of the shire, not as Chief Justiciar.

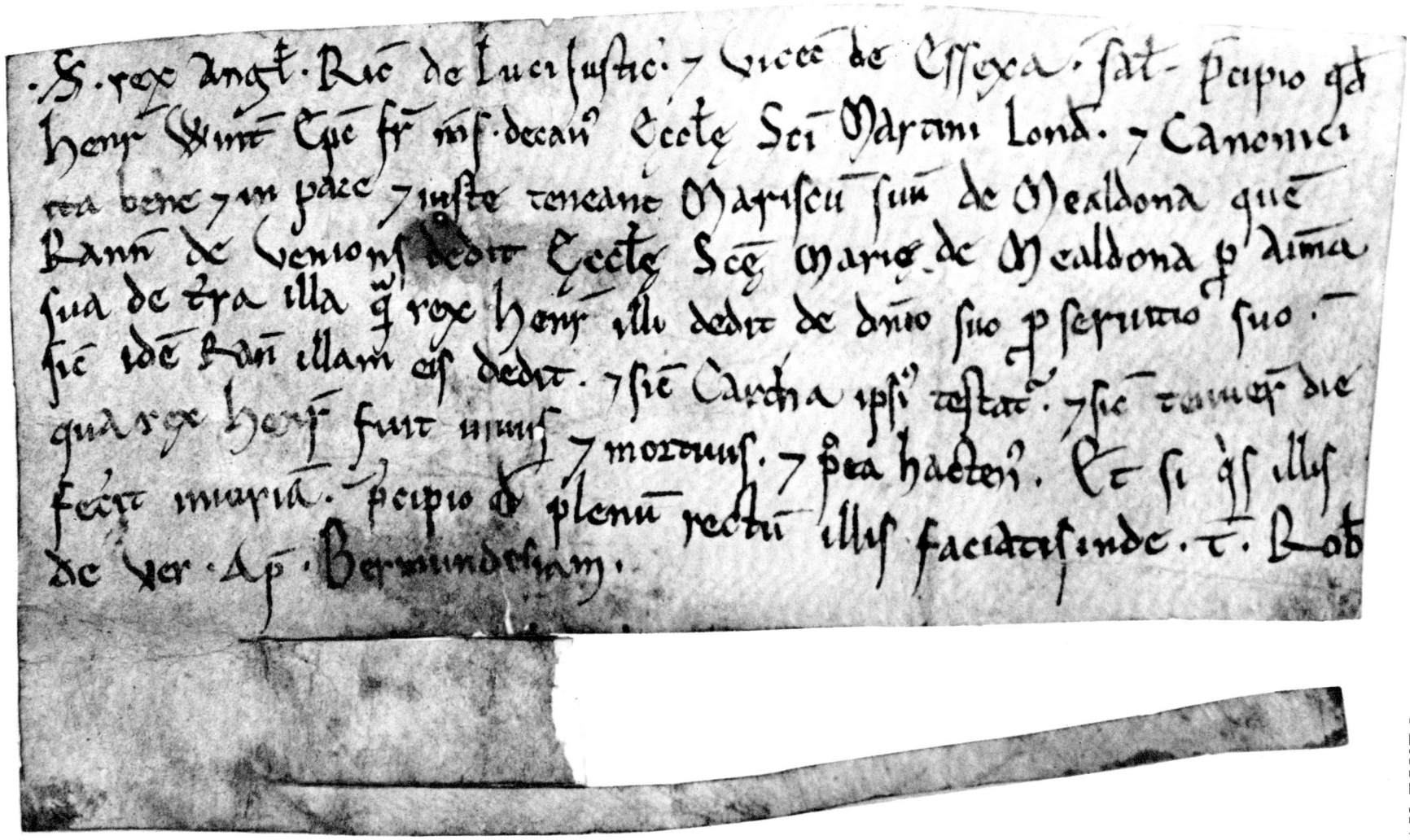

PLATE XVII

(London, The British Museum, Cotton Charter XVI. 34)

No. **500**

Date: 1135–6, at Westminster.

King Stephen confirms to Holy Trinity Priory, Aldgate, the pension of £25 *ad scalam* per annum from the revenues of the late Queen (Edith) Matilda in Exeter and orders the sheriff, whoever he may be, to make the payment at the accustomed times.

This writ in the hand of Scriptor XVI was damaged in the Cottonian fire but still remains largely legible. The tongue and seal are missing. The wording follows that of a previous writ of Henry I,[1] save in the name of the sheriff and the description of Queen Matilda as *conjugis mee*. The injunctive clause does not take the same form as in **501**, which also concerns a money payment and reads: *Et volo et precipio quod ecclesia predicta et canonici hos prefatos c solidos teneant et habeant imperpetuum.* In the present writ a technically necessary confirmation is combined with a *liberate* for the sheriff, which was also probably necessary at the beginning of a new reign.

[1] *Regesta* ii, 1493.

PLATE XVIII

(London, The Public Record Office, D.L. 10/12)

No. **389**

Date: 1136–March 1137, at Fareham.

King Stephen confirms to Miles of Gloucester the lands of Edric son of Chetel.

Written in the hand of Scriptor XVII, with a good impression of Stephen's First Seal in white wax on the tongue, this writ, addressed for Gloucestershire, serves a dual purpose. It confirms the land of Edric son of Chetel to Miles, as King Henry I granted it to his father, Walter; and it is also a writ of intendence (*Et omnes . . . tenentes intendant Miloni sicut domino suo*). It includes both a dispositive and an injunctive clause, but there is no unnecessary elaboration.

PLATE XIX

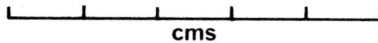

cms

a (Oxford, The Bodleian Library MS. Charters. Glouc. a. 1. 6)

No. **346**

Date: 1135–9, without place-date.

King Stephen orders that all the livestock (*pecunia*) of the Abbey of St. Peter of Gloucester, the abbot and monks go free of toll and all custom everywhere.

    This writ (*precipio*) seems to be written in the hand of Scriptor XVII. It is addressed in an unusual form to justices, sheriffs, barons, and officials (*ministri*) French and English, without mentioning any specific shire or shires, or whether it is for all England. In lines 3 and 4 the clause announcing the customary £10 penalty for unwarranted interference with the rights of the beneficiaries is clumsily drafted. The omission of the place-date has already been noted. In all, it is a careless and inefficient piece of draftsmanship. As one would expect in a simple writ of this kind, there is only one witness, but a man of importance, especially in Gloucestershire and Herefordshire.

b (London, The Public Record Office, E. 40/15395)

No. **445**

Date: Dec. 1135–Aug. 1139, at Beckenham (Kent).

King Stephen quitclaims the Priory of St. Pancras of Lewes of lot and scot, pleas, plaints, hustings, and all other liabilities, except *murdrum* and *latrocinium probatum*, in respect of lands which they have both in London and outside the *port* but within the shrievalty.

    The writ is in the hand of Scriptor XVII. It is, naturally, addressed to the authorities of London (Andrew *Bucca Uncta* being the justice). It contains, somewhat unusually (though there are other examples) a dispositive clause only, following the superscription, address, and salutation. It is more usual, in circumstances of this kind, to find a writ the text of which consists of an injunctive clause alone. A single witness, frequently of high rank, is usual in such writs as this.

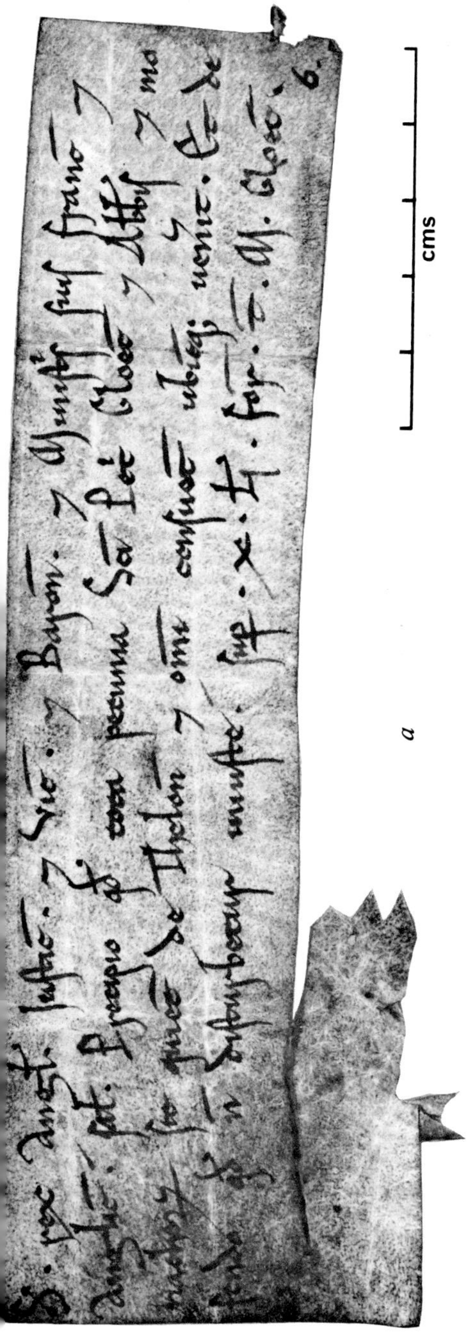

PLATE XX

cms

6.

a

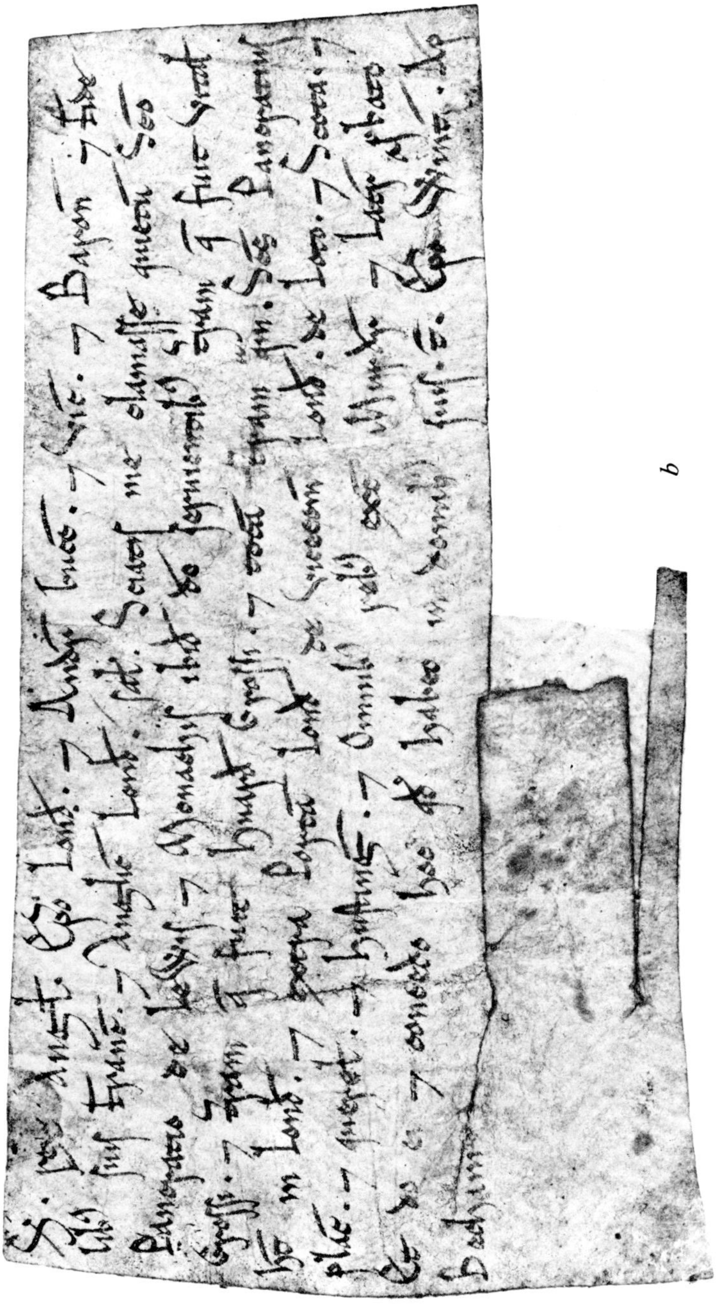

b

(London, The Public Record Office, D.L. 10/20)

No. **312**

Date: Dec. 1137, at Marlborough.

King Stephen confirms to Roger, son of Miles of Gloucester, and his wife Cecilia all the lands of Payn fitzJohn and all the lands which Payn gave Cecilia, his daughter, as her marriage portion and every agreement which Payn made with Roger when he married his daughter.

This royal confirmation, written in the hand of Scriptor XVIII, is a record in full writ-charter form. The seal is missing. It is addressed generally for England. The dispositive clause sets out the necessary details of the inheritance, the *maritagium* and the property acquired by purchase (*de acatis*); the injunctive clause includes the old traditional formulas. It seems to be a blanket confirmation of the most comprehensive kind, but Payn's widow, Sibilla, seems to have found some grounds to dispute the settlement with her son-in-law and daughter.[1] The whole document, which deals in detail with the marriage settlement and the inheritance of a daughter of a baronial magnate and former *curialis* and with the provision made for his widow, is of considerable interest to social historians.

In the dispositive clause the very emphatic words (lines 3–4) *in feodum et hereditatem hereditarie omnem hereditatem et omnia acata* seems to imply a clear distinction between inherited property and property acquired by purchase and untrammelled control over the latter. Judging from No. **313** we think it possible that Payn fitzJohn's widow argued that lands which her husband had acquired *de acatis* ought not to go with the inheritance to his daughter and that the judgment of the Curia Regis went against her.

[1] See No. **313** and Pl. L, a writ of Roger, Bishop of Salisbury, in his capacity as Chief Justiciar.

PLATE XXI

H. rex Angl' archiepis' episc' abbatibus comitib' justic' baronib' vicec' ministr' 7 omnib' fidelib' suis francis 7 angl' toci' angl' sal'. Sciatis me reddidisse 7 concessisse Rogo filio Milonis Gloec' 7 Cecilie uxori sue filie Pag' fil' Iohis in feod 7 heredita-
tem hereditarie omne hereditate' 7 oia acata ipsi Pag' que ipse tenebat die qua
fuit uiuus 7 mort' de queq tenuisset. Et omne mariagiu qd Pag' dedit filie sue
de honore Hug' de Lacero in t'ris 7 militib'. Et omne illud mais qd ipse Pag' habebat
in toto honore Hug' de Lacero sic' ipse Pag' debt 7 concessit illi ipsi Rogo cu filia sua
De acatis suis h' subscripta Maria scil' Bramfeld cu omib' suis pertinenc' ad dare illis in
elemosina. Et Wltecota ad tenend de canone Sci Almund' ex c' reddend' inde ꝑ annu'.
Et serui' Hug' de Canceles. Et feod Ase de Sceldestona. Et feod Butellarii. Et Esseford'
ad tenend de Hug' fil' Osb'. Et Suineercona de Rogo fil' Bren' Et Eckenesfeld
qd dedi ei in escambio de Lantilio. 7 de firma de Grosso monte cu omib' que ad illa ꝑ-
tinet. 7 nominatie cu nemore de Orcop. 7 cu landa de Garou. 7 traheren. 7 cu nemore de Harewuda. Et Fronta. 7 Dilun cu serui' Gaufr' russi. 7 t'ra de Cherlaua. Et
Dilun de Ht'o fil' Walt'. Et Ailenecota. 7 uinea Manordine cu t'ra 7 serui' Walt'
de Huges'. 7 Rogo de Liberdic' ad tenend de Suone parvolp'. De Charrac'. Butterlega. 7
Ailenecona. 7 In Wicha ꝑc' liberatur'. De milit'. Walteru' fil' herein' cu feod' .v. militu'.
7 herem' de Egelwart' c' .j. milit'. Et Anfr' de Euilardeuilla .v. milit'. Et feod'
Hug' Puhet de .v. milit' si eos debet. Sin' ad efficiend' de remanere honore.
Et Gardinu' de Hereg' qd rex h'r ei dedit. Et ꝑ hoc acatu' Pag' dedit Sibille
uxori sue in dote' de hereditate sua ut illud teneat ipse Sibilla de Rogo 7 Cecilia
uxore sua et ꝑ hoc de Westeling' et omib' suis ꝑtinenciis. Qr nolo 7 firmit' qd teneat bn' i'
bosco 7 plano 7 ꝑtis 7 pasturis 7 aquis infra burgu' 7 ext' in uiis 7 semitis 7 omibus
consuet' cu qd Pag' meli' tenuit hec igit' ꝑdicta 7 omem conuentione' q' ipse
Pag' fecit ꝑdicto Rogo cu filia sua concedo 7 confirmo ipsi Rogo 7 uxori
sue. T'. Aal' regina. 7 G' com' de Warr'. 7 Walt' marescall'. 7 Philippo de
Belmeis. apd Marleberam.

(20.)

PUBLIC
DUCHY
OF
LANCASTER
RECORD OFFICE

(London, The British Museum, Additional Charter, 19584)

No. **690**

Date: 1139–40, at Norwich.

King Stephen confirms to Reading Abbey lands in Windsor (Berks.) and Catshill (Surrey) in frankalmoign.

This charter is written in the hand of Scriptor XVIII. It has a bottom fold with a single slit for a seal-tag instead of the tongue and wrapper which were still in more general use in the royal Scriptorium. It is a record of a final concord *coram rege* between Ralph Purcell and the monks of Reading (*sicut inde finivit coram me cum ipsis monachis*—lines 7–8). It is in full writ-charter form addressed generally for England. The text includes a dispositive and an injunctive clause with traditional formulas and there are seven witnesses. In line 9 the word *teneant* has been interlineated. In a compromise action such as this the guarantee of a royal charter was still preferable to a bipartite indenture or chirograph. The tripartite chirograph was first used in 1195 and in that year began the great series of Feet of Fines, the retention of the *pes* in the Treasury providing the best available guarantee against forgery.

PLATE XXII

(Keele University, Hatton Wood Collection, 708)

No. **963**

Date: 1135–40, at Northampton.

King Stephen orders that the monks of Worcester Cathedral Priory are to hold their land of Boraston (Salop) as their benefactors (named) gave it them, and it is not to be distrained upon and it owes suit to no hundred, but only to the hall-moot of Burford (Salop).

This writ is in the hand of Scriptor XVIII and seems to have borne on the tongue a fragment of the forged First Seal of Stephen, which is now detached. Not only so, but the document has been tampered with, as may easily be seen. At the end of line 6 and the beginning of line 7, the words *Vel debito nisi sint plegii vel conventionatores* have been written over an erasure. A similar writ of Henry I, of which there is a copy in the Worcester Cartulary, has, at the equivalent point in the text, the words *nisi pro suo proprio* which, in the hand of Scriptor XVIII, would probably have fitted very well into the space of the erasure. The royal scribe was probably not implicated in the use of the forged seal, which may have been supplied by the tamperer in place of a genuine seal, which had been broken. Worcester Cathedral Priory certainly had access to the matrix of the forged First Seal, since it was also affixed to the *pancarte* confirmation (**964**) which they were alleged to have had from Stephen.

This writ (*precipio*) is addressed for Herefordshire and Shropshire and looks as if it had resulted from a judicial decision in favour of the monks, which presumably precluded any intervention by the shire courts addressed. In writs of this sort the old, traditional formulas are notably absent and there is only one witness, a member of the royal household.

PLATE XXIII

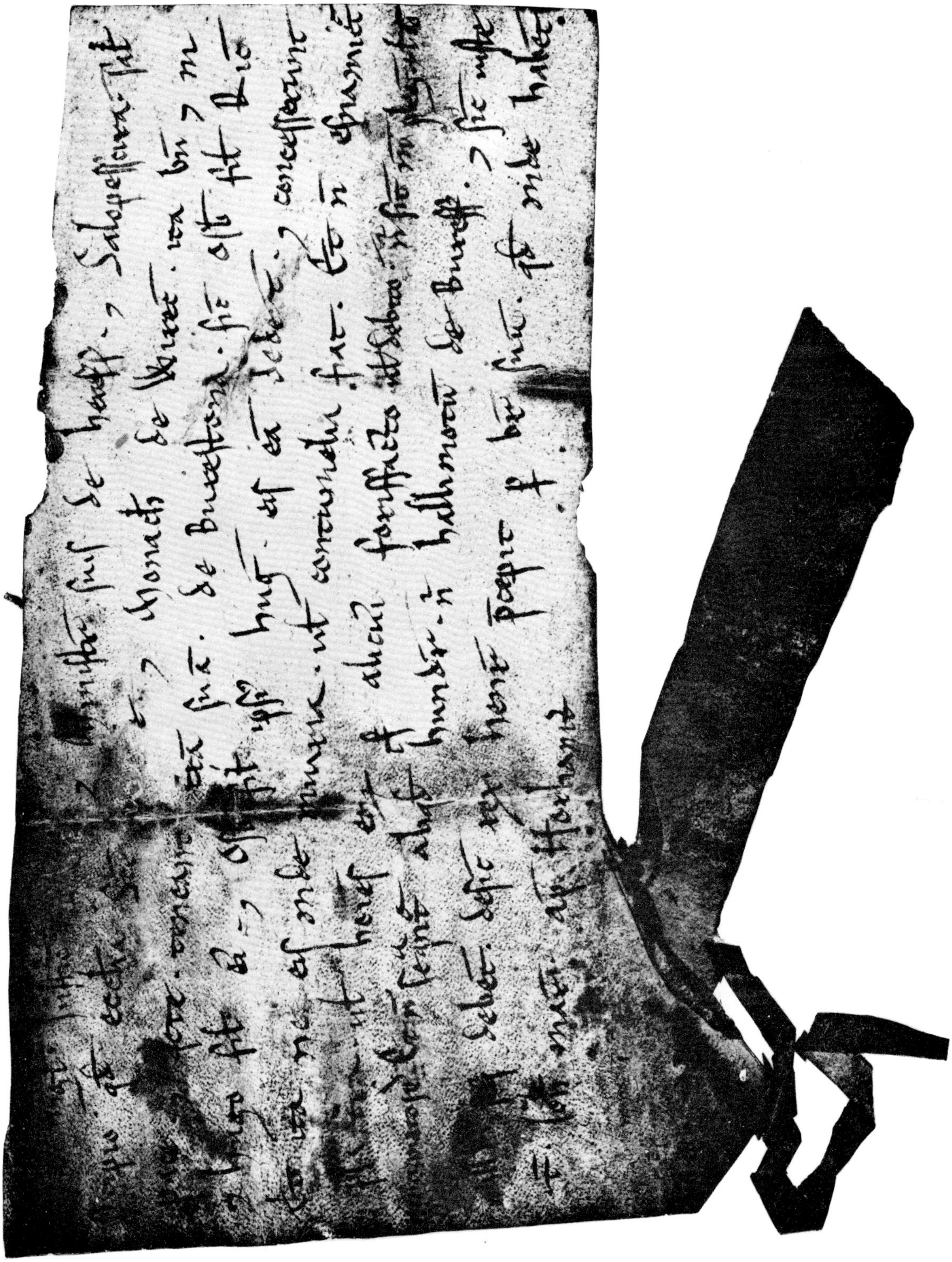

(London, The British Museum, Harleian Charter, 43. C. 13)

No. **114**

Date: Dec. 1140–Jan. 1141, at Lincoln.

King Stephen grants to Bordesley Abbey all the land of Bordesley and all the demesne land of Bidford (Warwickshire) except the land held by the villeins of that vill.

Written in the hand of Scriptor XVIII, this charter bears, on a tag passed through a slit in the bottom fold, a fragment of Stephen's Second Seal. This is important because it is one of the three certain examples of the use of this seal before the battle of Lincoln and the king's captivity, the others being **273** and **493**.

The charter is addressed generally for England. The 'movent' includes (lines 3–4) *pro incolumitate tocius regni mei*, which is not very frequently used in Stephen's charters. This is, in fact, a writ-charter of a formal type tricked out with the traditional formulas in the dispositive and injunctive clauses. The reference (lines 5–6) to the demesne land held by the *villani* is of some interest.

PLATE XXIV

(London, The Public Record Office, D.L. 10/14)

No. **437**

Date: 1140–4 (probably 1140), at Newton.

King Stephen grants to Robert, earl of Leicester, hereditarily the borough, castle, and county of Hereford.

The significance of this charter has been much discussed. G. H. White (*T. R. Hist. S.* 4th ser. xiii (1930) 72 ff.) believed that it was not the grant of an earldom, but in our opinion it represents the norm for the grant of a second county to a man who was already earl of one (Davis, *King Stephen*, 140). As the king's representative and military commander in the county, Earl Robert was apparently instructed to take over the land of the king's enemies, the few tenants-in-chief who were still loyal to Stephen being named; and there is the special case of Gotso of Dinan (lines 8–9).

The charter is witnessed by four earls and several important royal followers besides the Chancellor. For such a document it is not at all elaborate either in external appearance or in diplomatic composition. The seal, for example, was on a tongue, not on cords or a tag threaded through a bottom fold as in the grant of the Earldom of Essex to Geoffrey de Mandeville (**273**). This charter was written by Scriptor XIX, whose hand somewhat resembles that of Scriptor XX. Much of the dispositive clause is necessarily devoted to an enumeration of lands excepted from the grant, but otherwise it is very concise. The injunctive clause carefully and correctly refers to the grantee and his heirs after him (line 9) and the old traditional formulas are employed without any elaboration.

PLATE XXV

cms

(Évreux, Archives de l'Eure H (Supplément) Abbaye du Bec)

No. **74**

Date: 1136–9, at Marlborough.

King Stephen grants to the Abbey of Bec one hundred solidates of land annually in the manor of East Hendred (Berks.), which are over and above the £20 which he gave to Reading Abbey for the soul of King Henry.

These two fragments written in the hand of Scriptor XIX were found in a nineteenth-century binding. The text printed in *Regesta* iii, **74** has been restored from the transcript of the charter in Paris, Bibliothèque Nationale, MS. Lat. 13905 f. 21v. Only the corroboration or warranty clause calls for comment, since it is of a kind more common, perhaps, in continental than in English documents.

PLATE XXVI

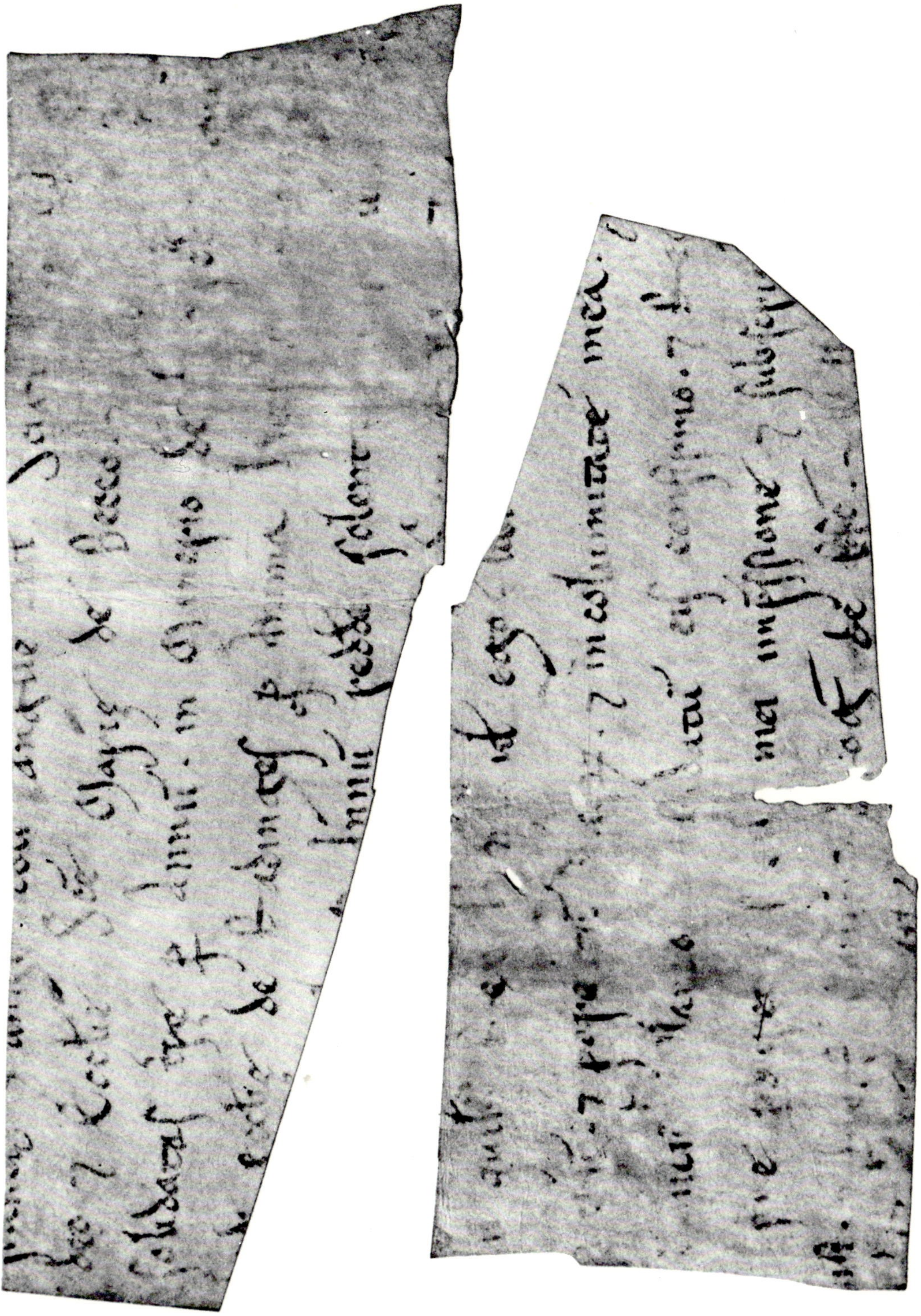

a (London, The Public Record Office, D.L. 10/13).

No. **390**

Date: 1136–June 1139, at Oxford.

King Stephen confirms to Miles of Gloucester hereditarily the land in Gloucestershire which he had obtained from the Bishop of Exeter. Cf. Pl. XIII.

Since the beneficiary is Miles of Gloucester, who deserted Stephen in September, 1139, 'R the chancellor' must be Roger le Poer and not Robert de Gant. The importance of this is that it shows that the writer, Scriptor XX, was working in and learned the practice of the royal Scriptorium before the arrest of the bishops. He was still in the royal service at least as late as *c.* 1144–5. His draftsmanship, as in this example, was always businesslike and brief.

b (Ely Cathedral, Muniments of the Dean and Chapter, Charter 8)

No. **266**

Date: 1144–5, at Bury St. Edmund's.

King Stephen orders that the monks of Ely hold their lands as well and fully as they held them when Bishop Nigel set out for Rome.

This writ-charter, addressed generally for England as for a confirmation, is written in the hand of Scriptor XX. It is a straightforward, brisk, and businesslike piece of draftsmanship, with a minimum of verbiage. Its purpose was clearly to safeguard the lands of the Cathedral Priory from encroachments in the absence of the bishop.

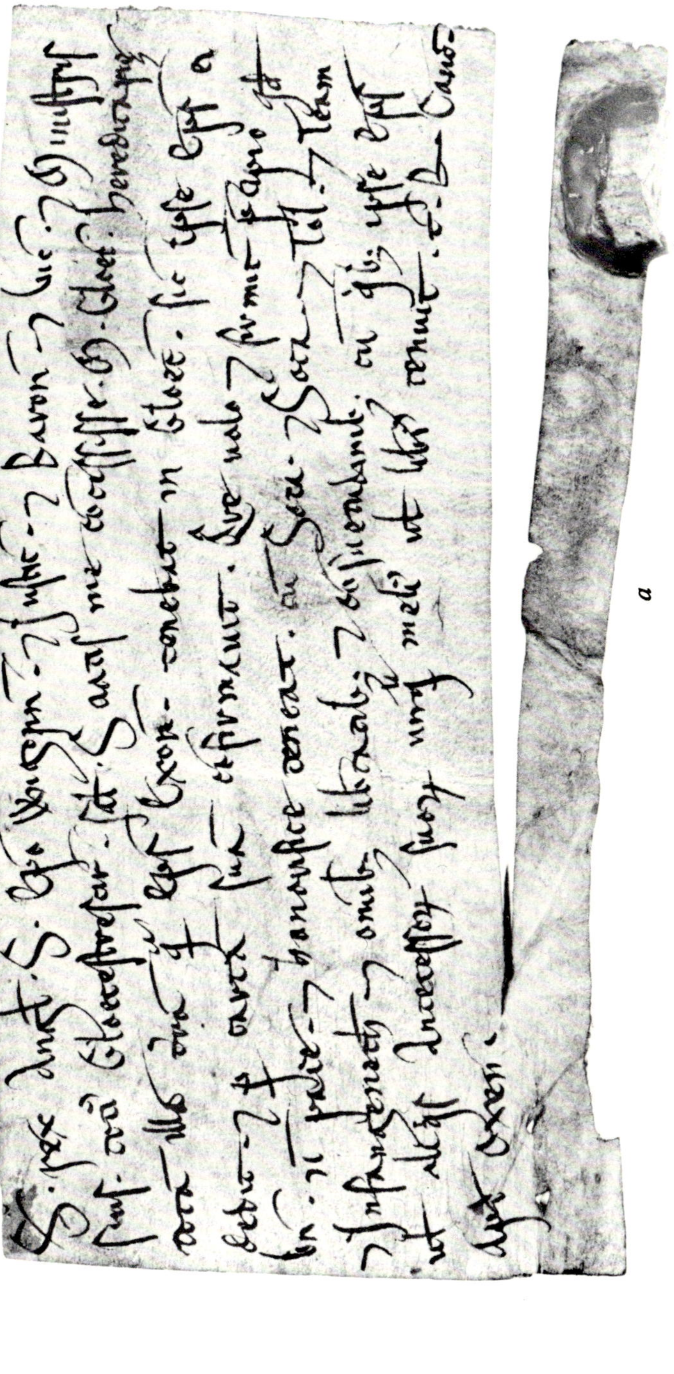

PLATE XXVII

a

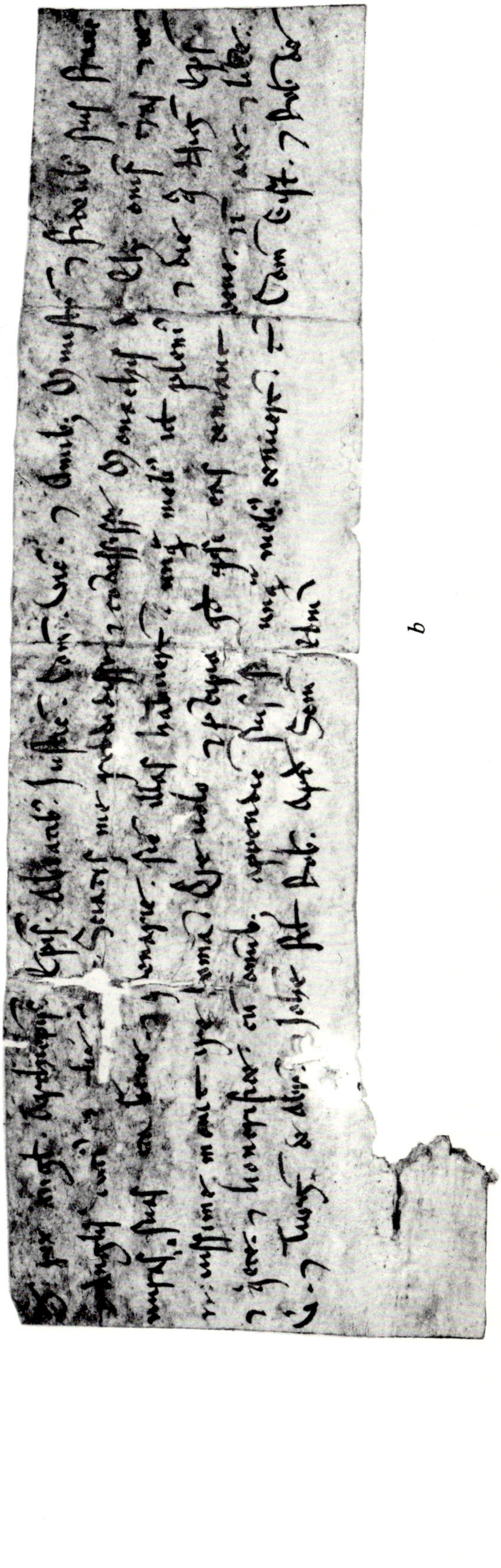

b

a (London, The Public Record Office, E 40/6987)

No. **517**

Date: 1135–54, at Westminster.

King Stephen has confirmed to the Priory of Holy Trinity, Aldgate, the land of Clayhurst at an annual rent of 5s. and Estmund's land at a rent of 8s. 6d.

Written in the hand of Scriptor XX (with underlinings by a later hand), this writ is addressed to the king's men of Beckenham (Kent). Surprisingly, for so concise a writ, it contains both a dispositive and an injunctive clause. The latter is carelessly drafted, the verb *teneant* being used twice (line 5). This bears all the marks of a hastily written document, in handwriting as well as in composition. The general marks of suspension and abbreviation above the line tend to come a trifle late, as though the scribe's pen had been moving quickly. There is nothing in this writ to enable it to be dated otherwise than by the limits of the reign.

b (Belvoir Castle, MSS. of the Duke of Rutland, Acle No. 699)

No. **176**

Date: 1139–54, at Westminster.

King Stephen grants to William de Chesney and his heirs the manor of Acle (Norfolk) with its appurtenances and its liberties as when it was in the king's hands.

Written in the hand of Scriptor XX, this is addressed for the shire court of Norfolk. The dispositive clause is austerely concise but the injunctive clause contains the customary traditional formulas. Scriptor XX gives, as he invariably does, the impression that his pen did not dawdle over the parchment and that he did not spin out his work beyond what was needful.

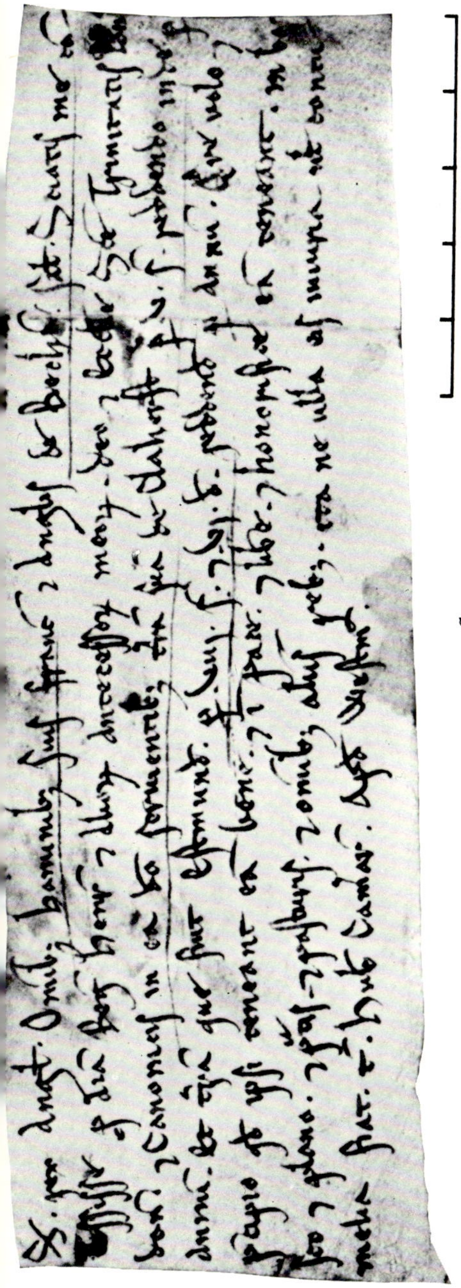

PLATE XXVIII

a

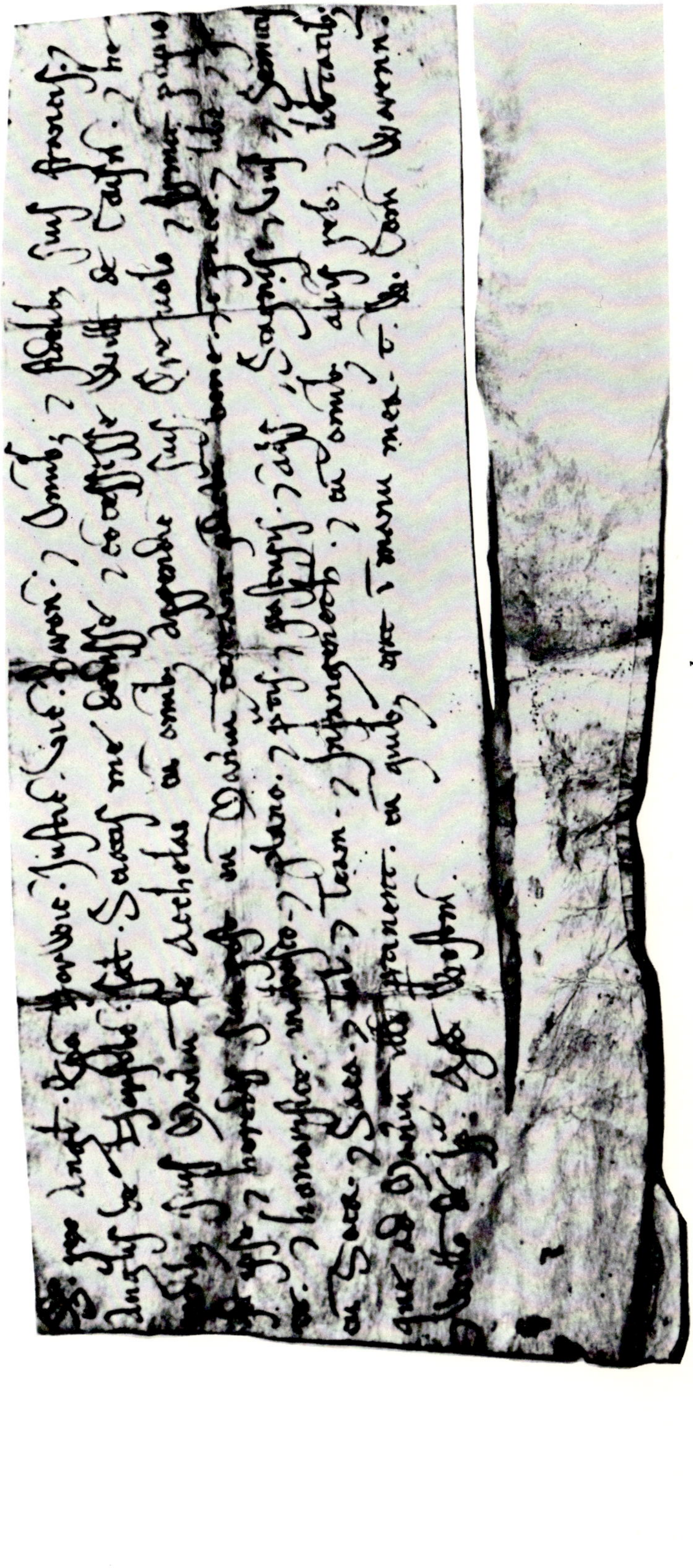

b

cms

a (Paris, Archives Nationales, K 23, no 23?)

No. **801**

Date: 1135–43, at London.

King Stephen grants to the monks and abbot of Savigny and their men freedom from tolls etc. in England on goods which they vouch for as their personal property.

 This writ seems to be in the hand of Scriptor XXI. It is very concise and addressed only to sheriffs and officials throughout England, that is, to those who were directly concerned with financial matters such as tolls. The text consists of an injunctive clause which is characteristic of this very common kind of writ. The £10 forfeiture is also a characteristic feature and likewise the single witness.

 The document, which was kept in the archives of the Abbey of Savigny until the French Revolution, must be earlier (probably much earlier) than 1143, when Stephen lost this part of Normandy.

b (London, The Public Record Office, E 327/254)

No. **177**

Date: 1149–53, probably *c*. Dec. 1153, at Eye.

King Stephen grants to William de Chesney in fee and inheritance specified tenures in exchange for Mileham, on condition that, if William or his son succeed in recovering Mileham, Stephen or his son shall have these specified lands back in their demesne.

 This writ (*sciatis*) in the hand of Scriptor XXI, has only a dispositive, and no injunctive, clause. It is in fact a notification to the relevant shire courts, those of Norfolk and Suffolk, of an agreement between the king and a local magnate who was an adherent of his. It shows Stephen thinking in the kind of feudal terms which characterize his treaty with Duke Henry. It is interesting that abbots, earls, and lieges (*fideles*) are included in the address in addition to the bishop, justice, sheriff, barons, and officials (*ministri*) who normally figure in royal writs addressed to shires.

PLATE XXIX

a

1137

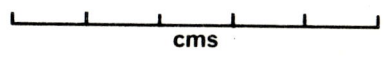

b

cms

(*Penes* Col. A. Gregory-Hood, Loxley Hall, Warwick)

No. **922**

Date: *c.* 1150, at London.

King Stephen confirms to Waverley Abbey the grant made by Simon, Earl of Northampton, of the manor of Combe (Warwickshire) for the building of an abbey of the same (Cistercian) Order.

We owe our knowledge of this charter to Sir Charles Clay, who noticed it hanging in the hall of Loxley Hall, Warwickshire. It has not previously been recorded. It is a good example of the hand and competent draftsmanship of Scriptor XXI. He begins the dispositive clause, as he commonly but not invariably does, with *sciatis quia* and this is followed by the present, not the perfect, tense. This clause includes a 'movent' whereby the royal family is associated with the benefaction. Here the king's sons, other than Eustace who is named individually, are referred to as *pueri*. Some other scribes habitually use *filii* in this context. In the injunctive clause the traditional formulas are included in the simplest form.

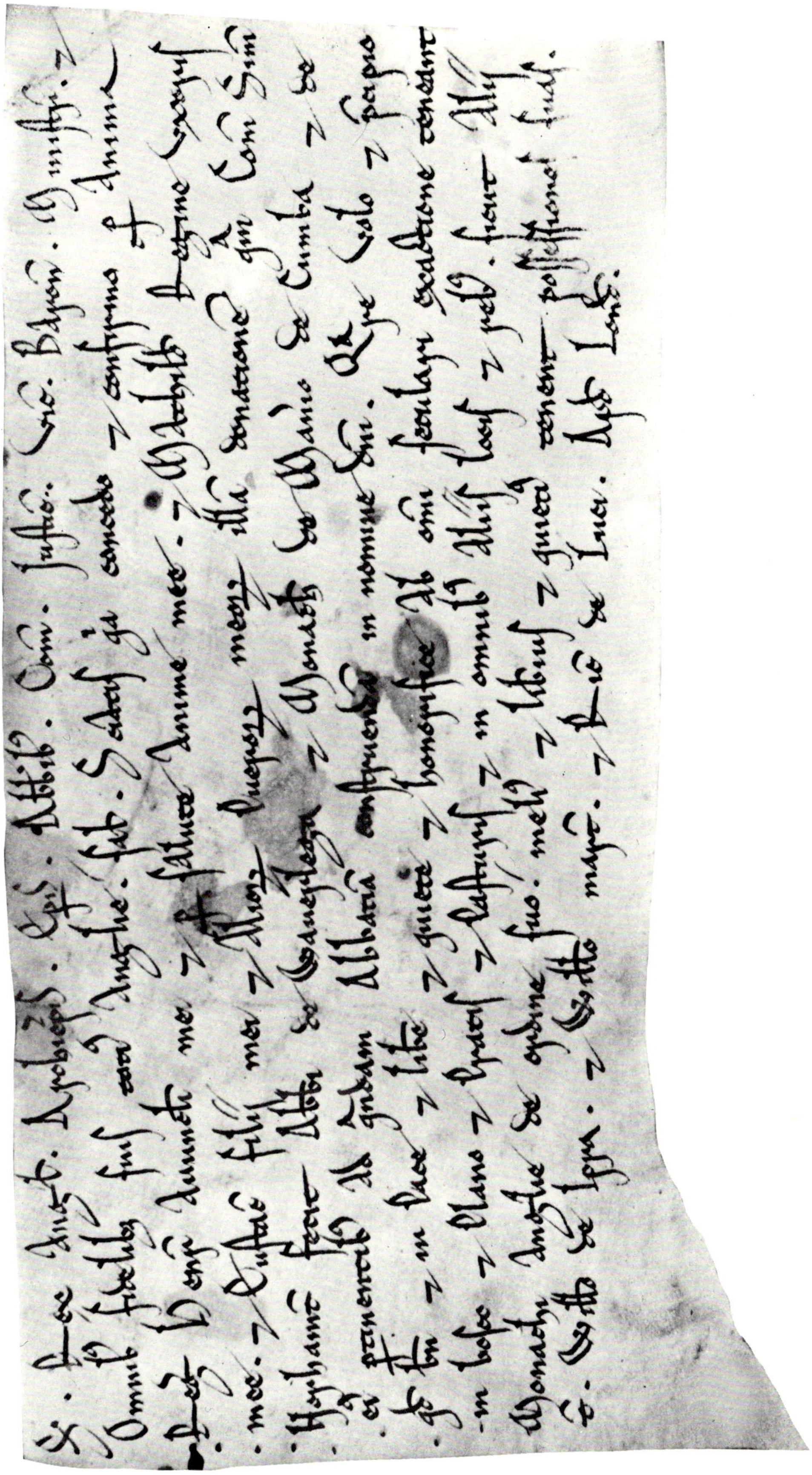

(The Shropshire Record Office, 972/14)

No. **460**

Date: Early in 1145, at Bury St. Edmunds.

King Stephen confirms to Lilleshall Abbey, at the request of Archdeacon Richard (Belmeis), prebends in St. Alcmund's, Shrewsbury.

This charter seems to be written in the hand of Scriptor XXI, a competent and concise draftsman who usually avoided all unnecessary elaboration, He tended, as here, to reduce the traditional mnemonic formulas to the barest minimum, using a phrase such as *et in omnibus aliis locis et rebus* (line 11) to cut them short. This, presumably, had become acceptable to the courts.

The attestation of the papal legate, Imar, Bishop of Tusculum, is a unique feature. As he remained in the country for only one or two months, his attestation dates the document firmly.

PLATE XXXI

S. Rex Angl̃: Archiep̃s. Ep̃is. Abbb̃. Comitib̃. Iustic̃. Vic̃. Baron. Ministr̃. ⁊ Omnib̃ fidelib̃ suis franc̃ ⁊ Angl̃is totī Angliē. sal̃t: Sciatis q̃a p̃ce R. ic Archidiac̃ dedi ⁊ concessi p̃ Animā Reg̃ Henr̃ Auunc̃ mei ⁊ Alior̃ p̃decessor̃ meor̃ Regū Anglie ⁊ p̃ salute mea ⁊ Mathilt Regine vxor̃s meē ⁊ Eustac̃ filij mei ⁊ Alior̃ pueror̃ meor̃ prebendā ip̃m Ricard̃ q̃m habuit in Ecclīā S̃ci Alchmund̃ de Salopesbia ⁊ totū dnium suū ⁊ om̃s Alias res suas Canonicis Regularib̃ de Dunmitona. ⁊ Om̃s Alias ꝓbendas p̃dicte Ecclīe S̃ci Alchmund̃ q̃ndo delib̃abunt. cū Omnib̃ ad illas p̃tinentib̃. Q̃re Volo ⁊ firmit̃ p̃cipio q̃ p̃dicti Canonici Regulares teneant ⁊ hant in p̃pe. ā Elemosinā b̃n ⁊ in pace ⁊ libe ⁊ q̃ete Ab om̃i sclari exactione. in bosco ⁊ plano. in p̃tis in pasturis. ⁊ in Omnib̃ Alijs locis ⁊ reb̃ sic̃ Elemosinam mea. T̃. Imaro Tuscul̃ Ep̃o legato. ⁊ R. heref̃ Ep̃o. ⁊ Rorb̃t eboric̃ Ep̃o. ⁊ R. de Gant Canc̃. ⁊ Com̃. W. de Warenn. ⁊ Com̃ Gisl̃ de Clara. ⁊ Com̃ Altico. ⁊ W. lorꝰ. ⁊ H. de Essex. Apd Scm Edm.

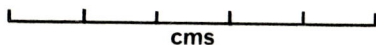

cms

(London, The Public Record Office, E. 40/6683)

No. **507**

Date: 1140–7, at London.

King Stephen restores to the Priory of Holy Trinity, Aldgate, its land in Smithfield which Earl Geoffrey of Essex had taken to make a vineyard.

This document, written in the hand of Scriptor XXI, is addressed for London and has both a dispositive and an injunctive clause with traditional formulas. There is a 'movent' (lines 3–5) and there are four witnesses, including the queen. These features give the document the appearance of a charter rather than a writ for execution of judgment. There is no reference to deraignment by the canons.

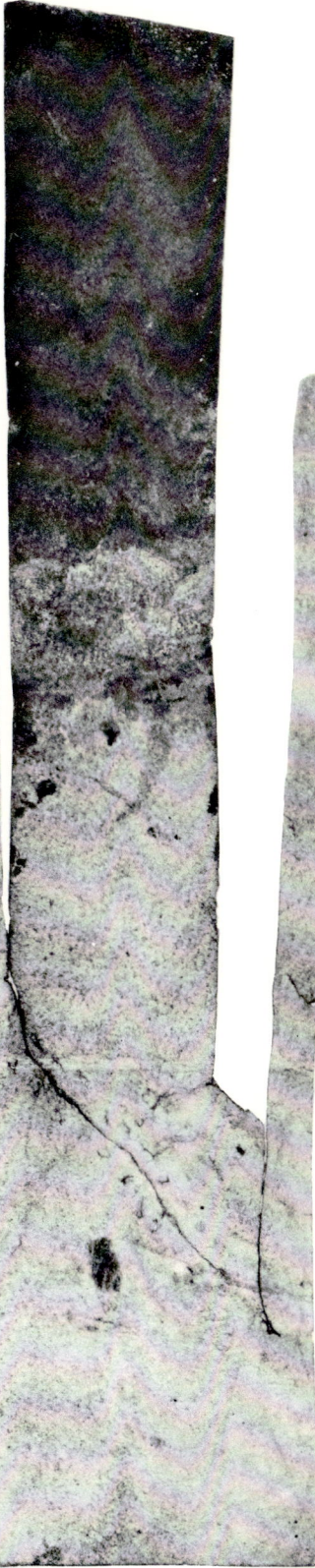

PLATE XXXII

(London, the British Museum, Additional Charter, 19582)

No. **689**

Date: 1139–53, at Reading.

King Stephen frees the land and men of Reading Abbey's manor of Rowington (Warwickshire) from Danegeld and all other exactions as they were free in the time of King Henry.

This brief injunction, written in the hand of Scriptor XXI, is addressed to the earl and officials (*ministri*) without any reference to the justice, sheriff, and barons of the shire. This is uncommon but it may be paralleled by the address to Waleran of Meulan, who was Earl of Worcestershire, in **966–7**. These earls were of the Beaumont family which was high in Stephen's favour before 1141. The present writ (like **966–7**) shows the earl actively involved in the administration of his shire. It must be subsequent to June 1139, because it bears Stephen's Second Seal.

PLATE XXXIII

H · Rex Angl' · R · Comitī Waṛbic̄ · ⁊ Ministr' suis · fac̄
Mando uob' ⁊ p̄cipio q̄d t̄ra ⁊ hōies Monacoꝛ Radīng de
Bochinrona sint tā ⁊ in pace ⁊ quieta de Danegeld
⁊ de omnib' aliis exactionib' · sicut fuerit quieta t p̄ Regis
Henr' · ⁊ sicut Carta Regis Henr' ⁊ mea eis testant̄ ·
⁊ Volo q̄ pacē habeano · T · R · de Luci · Apd Radīg

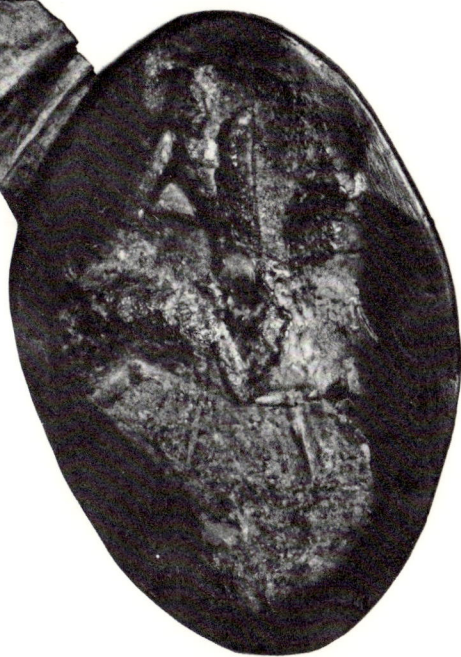

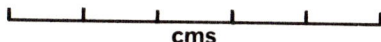
cms

a (Gloucester Cathedral Library, St. Peter's Abbey Deeds VI, f. 12)

No. **360**

Date: 1148–54, at Oxford.

King Stephen confirms the exchange between Gloucester Abbey and Walter, son of Richard, of Eastleach (Glos.) for Glasbury (Heref.)

This confirmation is written in the hand of Scriptor XXII, drafted in his workmanlike style and with a marked absence of verbiage or inflated formulation. The address begins as for the two shire courts directly concerned, namely those of Gloucestershire and Herefordshire, but concludes with the words *totius Anglie*. It is not clear to us whether there may have been a specific reason for such a form of address or whether it was a slip on the part of a hard-worked scribe, who was usually a careful draftsman.

b (London, The Public Record Office, E. 40/15389)

No. **448**

Date: 1148–53, at Lewes.

King Stephen confirms to Lewes Priory the gift of a fishery at Pevensey made to it by his son, Count Eustace.

This is written in the hand of Scriptor XXII, who also wrote **449** and **450** for St. Pancras of Lewes. It is addressed to the bishop, justice, sheriff, and officials (by which one would ordinarily understand a shire court) and all the king's lieges of the Rape of Pevensey. There is a minimum of detail and an absence of archaic phraseology in the drafting.

This should be compared with **449** (Pl. XXXV *a*). In external appearance the two charters, written by the same scribe for the same beneficiary on the same occasion (judging by the witnesses and place-date) are very much alike, but their drafting, though similar, is not precisely the same, even where it may seem that the same formulas would have served. This can be seen in the wording of the two dispositive clauses. The same applies to **450** (Pl. XXXV *b*).

PLATE XXXIV

H. Rex Angl. Epis et Justic. et Vic. et Baron. et Minist. et Omnib fidelib suis tot Angl. Sal. Sciatis me concessisse Escambiu illud qd Abbas Gist et Convent Gloecestr fecert cu Walt fil Ric de tra sua de Clasberia p tra eide Walt de Estleche. Ideo volo et firmit pcipio qd Monachi Gloecestr pdicta tra de Estlech bn et in pace et libe et quiete teneant et habeant cu omnib libtatib et litis consuetudinib eide tre ptinentib sic ide Walt eam illis concessit. T. R. Epo Linc. et Will de Caisn. et Jordan fil Tesc. Apd Oxen.

a

H. Rex Angl. Epo Cicestr et Justic. et Vic. et Baron. et Minist. et Omnib fidelib suis de Rapo Leuenesell. Sal. Sciatis me concessisse et confirmasse donatione illa qua Com Cust fil meus fecit Ecclie sci Pancratu de Lewes et Monachis in ea deo servientib de Piscaria de Leuenesell q est iuxta Langeneia et ptinentus eiusde Piscarie. Quare volo et firmit pcipio qd Ecclia illa et Monachi Piscaria illam bn et in pace et libe et quiete teneant cu ptinentus ei imppetua elemosina soluta et quieta omni sctatqz exactione et servicio sic fil meus Com Cust eis illis dedit et concessit et carta sua confirmavit. T. Will de Braiosa. et Rob de Hast. et Rog de firni. Apd Lewes.

b

cms

a (London, The Public Record Office E. 40/15443)

No. **449**

Date: 1148–53, at Lewes.

King Stephen confirms to Lewes Priory the gift of the service of the land of Robert of Horsted, made by his son, Count Eustace, and also gifts from the barons of the honour of Pevensey.

This confirmation is written by Scriptor XXII, who makes most of his general abbreviation signs in this document with a very small stroke. It is addressed as for a shire court, but the shire is not specifically named. The drafting, especially of the injunctive clause, is excellently concise, and no archaic or inflated formulas are employed. The word *exactione* (line 10) looks as though it had been 'improved', but clearly the meaning has not been altered. Compare Plate XXXIV *b* written by Scriptor XXII for Lewes on the same occasion and also Pl. XXXV *b*.

b (London, The Public Record Office, E. 40/6691)

No. **450**

Date: 1148–53, at Lewes.

King Stephen confirms to Lewes Priory an exchange (*commutationem et escambium*) which Bishop Roger [of Salisbury] made with the monks of land which belonged to Hervey of Wilton in Netheravon for two and a half hides of the chapelry of Pevensey, which the monks are to hold in frankalmoign, as this was confirmed by King Henry.

This charter, written in the hand of Scriptor XXII, is addressed generally for England. The text includes a dispositive and an injunctive clause and is a good example of this scribe's concise draftsmanship. The word *escambium* is commonly, and *commutatio* (line 3) rarely, used in this context in royal charters and writs. Compare Pls. XXXIV *b* and XXXV *a* written by the same scribe for the same beneficiaries on the same occasion.

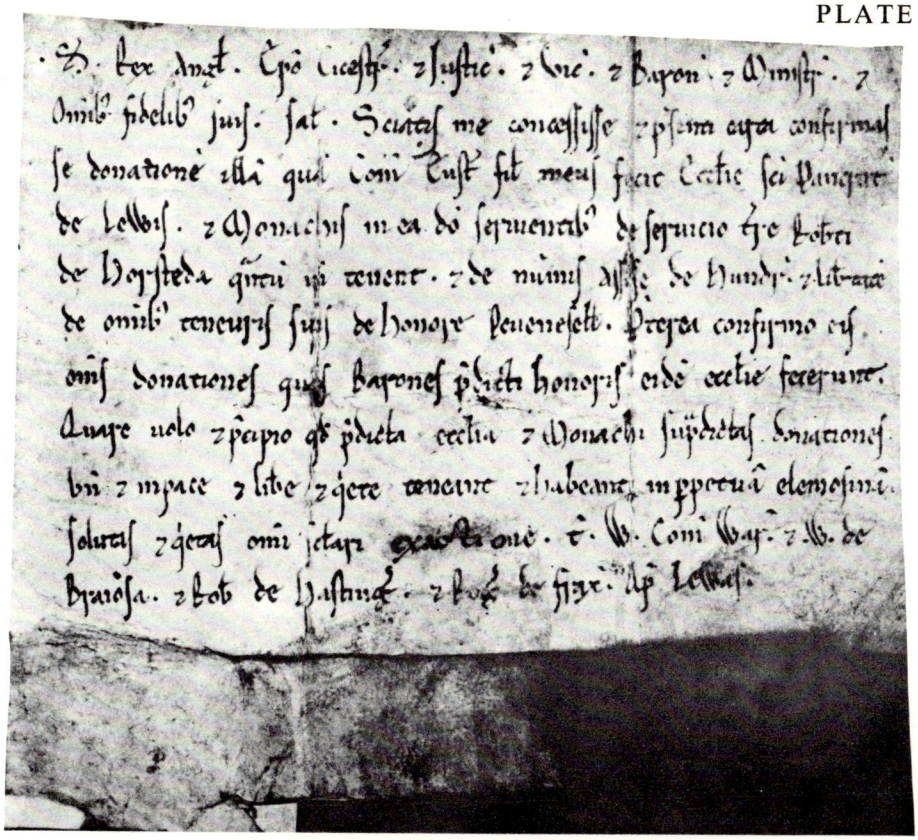

a

cms

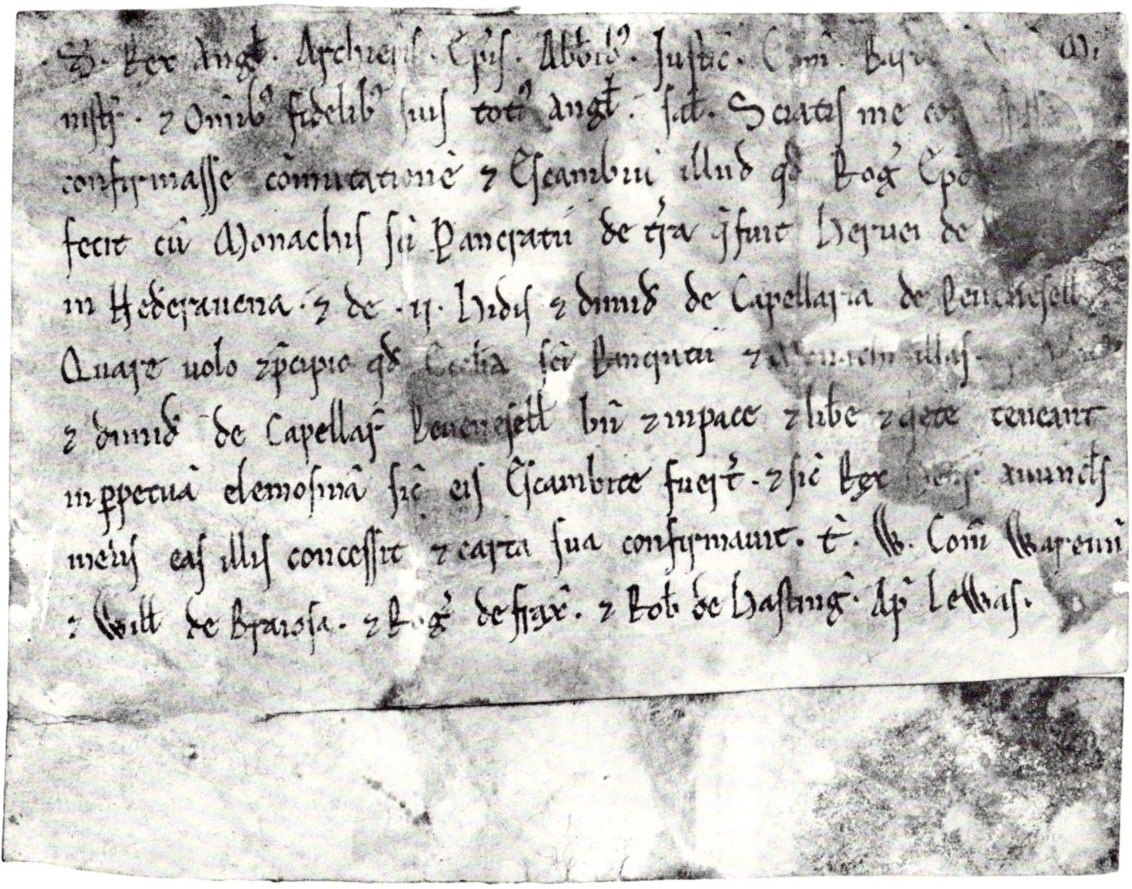

b

(London, The Public Record Office E. 40/14897)

No. **504**

Date: 1147–52, at Castle Hedingham.

King Stephen confirms to the Priory of Holy Trinity, Aldgate, the perpetual custody of the hospital by the Tower of London, given by Queen Matilda *coram rege* and also the mill by the Tower and its land and £20 per annum from the revenue of Edredeshythe, also given and confirmed by the queen.

This charter of confirmation, with its bottom fold and long parchment seal-tag, is in the hand of Scriptor XXII. The interesting feature of it is that, while the hospital is mentioned in the dispositive clause (line 4) the mill and the annual pension of £20 are introduced only in the injunctive clause (lines 6–8). We take the last sentence to mean that the canons might move the hospital to wherever should be most suitable for it to be established.

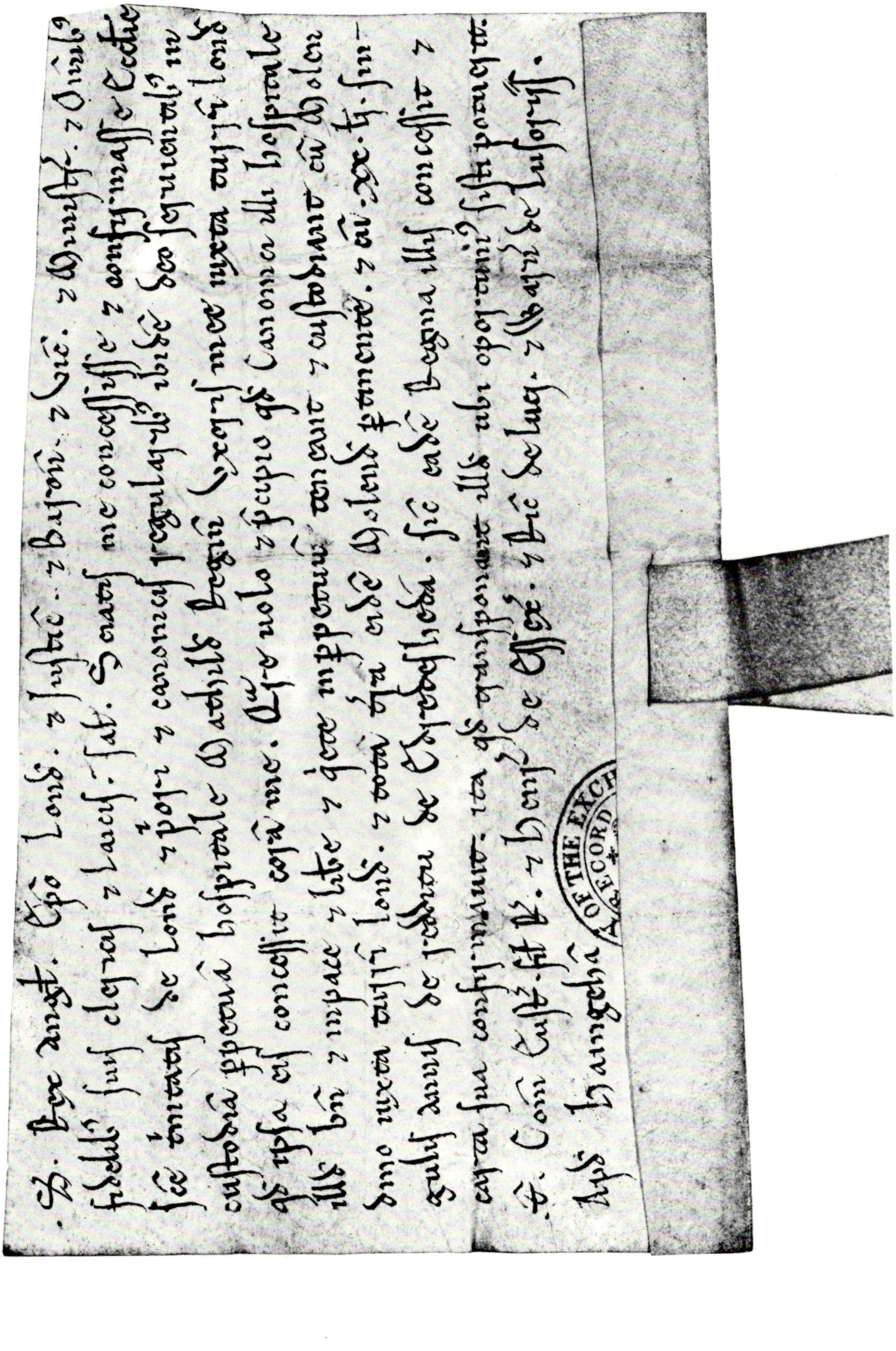
OF THE EXCH
RECORD

(London, The Public Record Office, E. 40/2021)

No. **515**

Date: 1136–54, at St. Albans.

King Stephen confirms to the Priory of Holy Trinity, Aldgate, the land of Barksdon given by Gervase of Cornhill and Richard, son of Hubert.

This charter of confirmation, being written by Scriptor XXII, may have been issued after 1146,[1] and the names of the witnesses would also suggest this, but we cannot be certain. It is a good example of the clear and uncomplicated draftsmanship of this scribe and comparison with his other products emphasizes the uniformity of his work.

[1] See *Regesta* iii, xv.

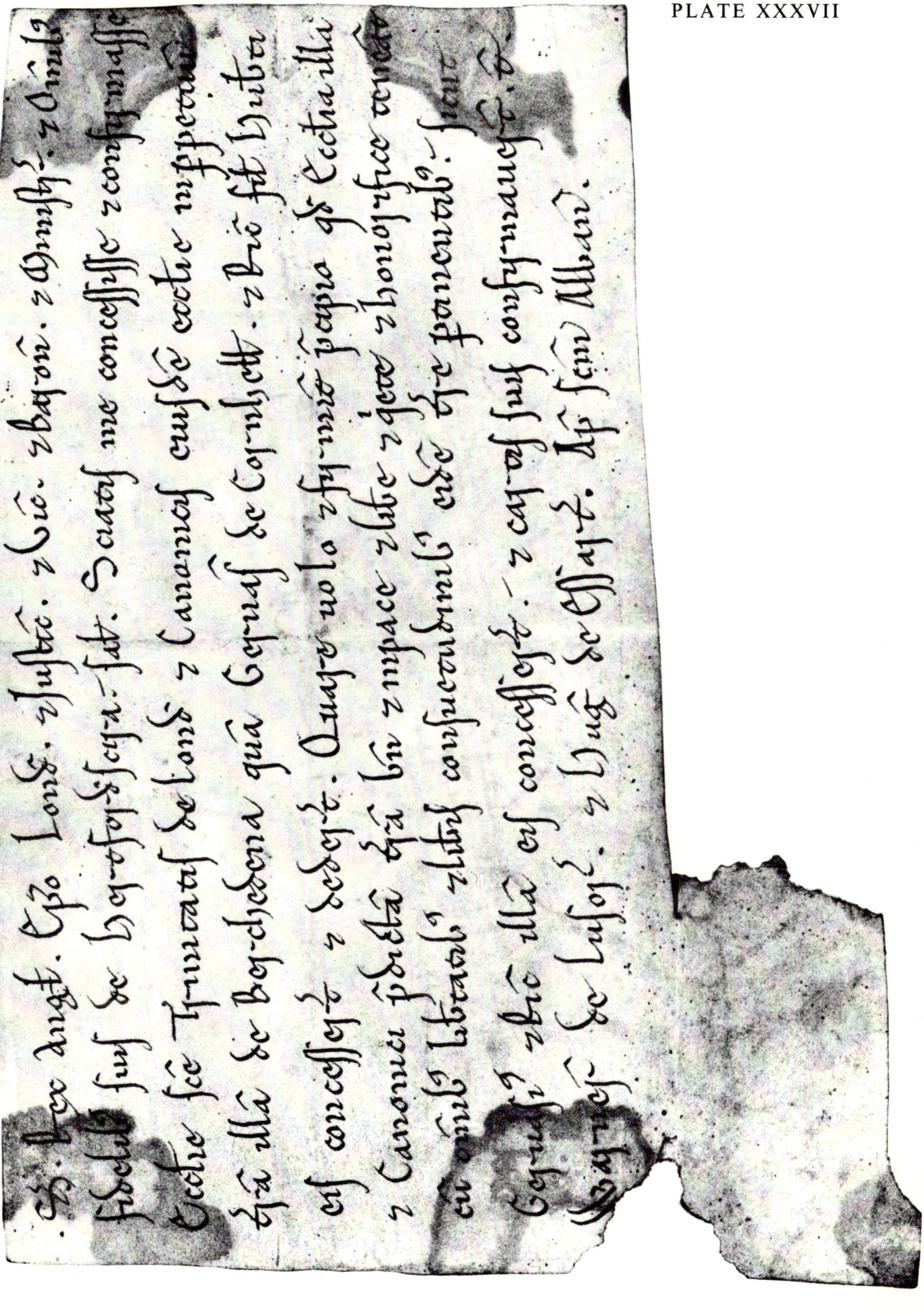

PLATE XXXVII

(Rouen, Archives de la Seine Mar., 8 H 108)

No. **77**

Date: 27 March 1149, at Le Bec.

Duke Geoffrey grants to the Abbey of Bec three prebends of Bures (Seine-Mar.) to hold freely and quit when they are relinquished by their present incumbents.

This charter is written by scribe **h** who wrote **443** in favour of the Abbey of Lessay,[1] the original of which was destroyed in 1944. The charter has a bottom fold and the Second Seal of Duke Geoffrey in green wax is appended on a tag. This is the only known example of the seal and its similarity to the Norman type of seal is noteworthy. The legends were read in the eighteenth century by D. Maur Andren as:[2]

S GOFFREDI DEI GRATIA [DUX] NORMANN[ORUM]
GOFFREDUS DEI GRACIA [COMES ANDE]GAVORUM.

The obverse or lance side represents Anjou and the reverse side represents Normandy.

The document is drafted with the clarity and conciseness characteristic of Norman charters. The text consists of a dispositive clause only and the archaic formulas commonly used in English charters are conspicuously absent. This charter is precisely dated, with a formula also used in **408** and **599.**

Among the witnesses are Richard the chancellor and Thomas the chaplain. The former is Richard de Bohun, chancellor of Normandy; the latter Thomas of Loches, chancellor of the Count of Anjou.[3] This is the only occasion upon which these two attest together and the titles they bear in this Norman charter are significant. It is clear that Geoffrey was careful to retain a separate chancellor for Normandy. The traditions and practice of the Norman Scriptorium exercised a very strong influence upon the scribes employed by Duke Henry before his accession to the English throne, for that seems to be where they learned their business. In Henry's English charters during this time we can see them trying to adapt themselves to English practice.

[1] C. H. Haskins, *Norman Institutions*, 138.
[2] L. Delisle, *Recueil des Actes de Henri II*, Introd., 135.
[3] See *Regesta* iii, xxxiii.

PLATE XXXVIII

a

(Rouen, Archives de la Seine-Mar. *7 H 12)

No. **304**

Date: 1144–50, at Rouen.

Duke Geoffrey and his son Henry confirm Abbot Henry de Sully in the rights of his abbey of Fécamp.

Henry, as heir in Normandy and heir to his mother's claims in England, issued a number of charters jointly with each of his parents. His dynastic position was thus fully recognized by participation in *acta* of this kind on formal occasions and for important beneficiaries.

This charter has a bottom fold with a single slot for the seal-tag .The scribe's hand, a clear and firm one which we have not identified, shows none of the signs of cursiveness which were becoming so obvious in the hands of scribes employed by Henry I and Stephen.[1] There are *ſt* and *ƀ* ligatures. The scribe has got some of his lines uneven (e.g. at *actoritate* (sic) and again at *abbati* in line 3) probably when he paused to adjust his parchment. The dispositive clause includes the words *et actoritate* (sic) *sigilli nostri confirmamus.* The brief injunctive clause introduced by *eapropter* (line 5) is followed by a sanction, namely enforcement of penalties laid down by Count Richard. The place-date *data carta ista apud Rothomagum* is less laconic than the English practice, which usually omits the first three words. The composition of the charter is subtly different from that of a charter written by an English *scriptor regis* at the same date, but it is clear that we are confronted not by two irreconcilable diplomatic traditions but by forms in which the resemblances are more striking than the discrepancies.

---

[1] Bishop, *Scriptores Regis*, 13.

PLATE XXXIX

.G. Dux nam̄ 7 Comes Ans̄ 7 b. filiꝰ ei̅ꝰ. b Archiepo Epō Brionib; 7 OmiꝬ viccomi
tib; 7 Ministrꝭ 7 fidelib; 7 Justeñs ſuis noꝭ añnꝭ Saℓ. Sciati q̄ ego 7 henricꝰ filiꝰ mꝭ
ꝰ Concedim̄ 7 Aℓcornccare ſigilli nꝛi confirmam̄ henrico Robano hſcorum 7 Ecclie iſsactorum
oms̄ Consuetudinꝭ ſuaſ 7 dignitaroſ intedẽf. i̅ꝗnꝛf. i̅agꝰf. i̅porꝛoloꝰ. ꝑlnꝰf. iꝑlaceneꝭ. 7 i̅
Omib; Aliꝰ redoꝰ ad Ecctiam ꝑtinentib; ſic Rreꝗ eǧꝛꝰ caꝗꝰ milatuꝛ ꝰia i̅drennuf. capꝭ
volo 7 ꝑcipio q̄ Ecctia teneat libe 7 qete 7 honoꝛfice abꝗ illa iqietacione ut i̅ nnirrnro
ne ſeculariꝰ ut Justeqꝛe poteſtatꝰ 7 fi alꝗf ſuꝗ boc alꝗꝬ ꝟumpſꝛ te. Ego capiä emendacionꝭ
ꝗa Comeſ Ricaꝛ̄ꝰ inſtituit te ut ego baioꝭ. Rte ego abiu̅ꝛ. Rte cardett. Ragⁱn de ſic
ⱬ auꝯ. Japiſteꝗo. Rot de nouo buꝛgo. Oſt de carhnu. Goſfꝛ debꝛnꝰ. Auaℓo ꝛonnaꝛ̄. Coſu
hꝛꝰ tꝛa. Ridello de redeno. Crⱬ̄gⱬano de Graſaℓubl. henꝛie deſuꝛꝛꝛꝛꝰ. laca bꝛra iſta apℓ
rocₕoñ.

PROPRIÉTÉ PUBLIQUE
SEINE-INFÉRIEURE

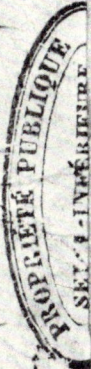

a (London, The British Museum, Harley Charter 84 C. 3)

No. **104**

Date: 1153–April 1154 (probably *c.* June 1153), at Leicester.

Duke Henry confirms the gift of Ernald de Bosco for the foundation of a Cistercian abbey at Biddlesden (Bucks.).

The lines of this charter are ruled, which is most unusual, and it is in the hand of Scriptor XXIII who was employed by Henry before his accession to the throne. He also wrote **180, 339, 379,** and **459** in the first seven months of 1153. One later charter in his hand has survived, written for Henry d'Oilly, which was given at the royal headquarters on a campaign in Wales and probably dates from 1157. From the latter charter it appears that the scribe was 'magister Radulfus clericus domini regis' and he may later have gained higher preferment. It is, however, significant that a scriptor should have been a *magister*.

The present charter is very much regal in form and tone, even referring (line 11) to *consuetudinibus corone mee pertinentibus*. In the 'general' address the scribe refers to *amicis et fidelibus suis Normannis et Anglis* instead of the more usual *Francis et Anglis*. The word *omnibus* at the beginning of the address was not usual in charters emanating from the royal Scriptorium. There appear to be several injunctive clauses: one beginning (line 6) *Quare firmiter precipio*; the second begins (line 9) *et volo et firmiter precipio* with a Tironian *et* and no capital letter; the third begins (line 11) *Et precipio*. These are trifling irregularities, if indeed they can be called 'irregularities' in view of the freedom enjoyed by scribes; but they are of a kind which, other things apart, would suggest that this scribe, competent though he was, had not obtained his experience in the English royal Scriptorium. A similar suggestion is conveyed by his painstaking hand. His work should be compared with that of Norman scribes.

b (Gloucester Records Office, D 471/T1/2)

No. **306**

Date: Aug. 1153–Apr. 1154, at Berkeley.

Duke Henry confirms to Nigel fitz Arthur, his wife and heirs, land in Combe in Wotton-under-Edge (Glos.) which Nigel had given to his wife in dower, for the service of half a knight, so long as he can guarantee it. If the Duke cannot guarantee it, a specified exchange from his demesne is to be given in lieu. In respect of the recognition of this gift, Nigel has paid the Duke 40 marks of silver and his wife has given a golden ring.

This charter is written in the hand of scribe g who wrote Duke Henry's charter relating to the Earl of Chester's compensation to Lincoln Cathedral (**492**).[1] There is a bottom fold with a parchment tag but no seal. The general address is preceded by the word *omnibus* in the manner of Scriptor XXIII, but this scribe uses the ordinary phrase *fidelibus Francis et Anglis* not *Normannis et Anglis*. There is no injunctive clause, but this record of agreement ends with a warranty clause in line 7: *pro posse meo rationabiliter guarantizabo*, which provides a necessary safeguard for the grantor in the word *rationabiliter*. The majority of the witnesses are members of the Duke's household, but Robert fitz Harding and his son Maurice had a direct interest in the agreement. It was not unusual for royal charters to include as witnesses persons who had a direct or indirect interest in the matters with which they deal, or who were influential local magnates. This, no doubt, served to commit them in some sort as accessaries to the *acta*.

---

[1] We are indebted to Mr. Bishop for this information. Facs. in *Reg. Antiq.*, ii, pl. xvi.

PLATE XL

a

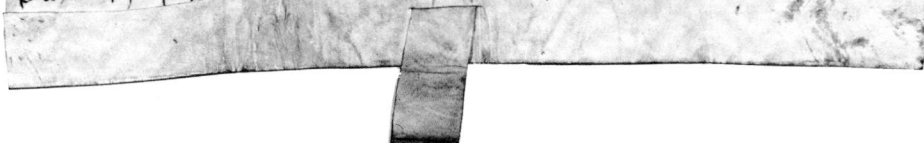

b

(Stafford, The William Salt Library, MSS. of the Marquess of Anglesey, no. 1577)

No. **459**

Date *c.* June–July 1153, at Warwick.

Duke Henry confirms to the Cathedral of St. Chad and Walter, Bishop of Lichfield, their assarts, in the Forest of Cannock, at Longdon (Staffs.) and in other forests, made before 1153.

This charter is written in the hand of Scriptor XXIII. In his 'general' address he includes significantly *amicis* before *fidelibus*, as he usually does, and adds *Normannis et Anglis* instead of the more usual *Francis et Anglis* of royal charters. In the injunctive clause he employs the uncommon form *in bona pace et quiete et libere et honorifice*. This or *in bono et pace* etc. is a small but characteristic trick of his style. Likewise *ne quis eis iniuriam vel molestiam aliquam vel dampnum aliquid facere presumat* is not exactly the form of words usually employed in the royal Scriptorium. We are again left with the impression that this scribe was not yet quite accustomed to English usage.

PLATE XLI

cms

(Exeter Cathedral Dean and Chapter MS. 2073)

No. **284**

April–21 Nov. 1136, without place-date.

Stephen confirms to Exeter Cathedral the churches of St. Petroc, St. Stephen etc.

This badly damaged document has been inexpertly mounted on vellum, perhaps as long ago as Dean Lyttelton's time. There is a note, which may be in his hand, saying: 'N.B. there was a seal appendant to this deed when I found it, but it was entirely decay'd and dropped from the body of the deed as soon as I touched it.' It is now impossible to see how this redundant seal might have been appended, whether on a tongue, on a tag, or on cords. There is no mention of a seal in the authenticating clause. The document purports to be a royal charter of confirmation in diploma form after the Old English (or old Norman) fashion, a rare thing indeed at this date[1] and an exceedingly unskilled piece of draftsmanship. It begins with an invocation. The superscription in which Stephen is described as *Willelmi Anglorum primi regis nepos totiusque Anglie rex ac moderator* is unique. There follows a formal 'movent' and another occurs at the end of the text. The dispositive part is quite explicit, but in the present tense, not, as in ordinary writ-charters, in the past tense. There is no injunctive clause and no anathema, but a clause of authentication reads: *Et ut hec ita data inviolabiliter et inconcusse sub eterno munimento permaneant signo Sancte Crucis consignata coram testibus subscriptis dimitto*. There are no *signa* and there is no trace of names having ever been inserted in the last five spaces of the left-hand column, where the clergy 'confirm'. In the right-hand column, the styles of the earls of Surrey, Northampton, and Buckingham are not those ordinarily used by the Earl of Warenne, Earl Simon (of Senlis), and Earl Giffard (of Longueville). None is impossible, but the conjunction of the three casts further suspicions upon a charter already suspect. Similarly, Roger, Bishop of Coventry, usually appears as Bishop of Chester. The ways of forgers are strange and there is no knowing why one of them should have adopted this outmoded form. Perhaps the diploma was written in good faith by an old-fashioned scribe employed by the beneficiaries, in the hope of having it authenticated when Stephen was besieging Exeter Castle in 1136, or the king may have made a formal grant orally on a public occasion (as the list of witnesses would suggest) leaving the onus upon the beneficiaries to procure an authenticated charter.

[1] Compare No. **345** (B.M. Cotton Ch. xvii. 3—badly damaged by fire) which is a spurious general confirmation for Gloucester Abbey, and **288** for Eye Priory.

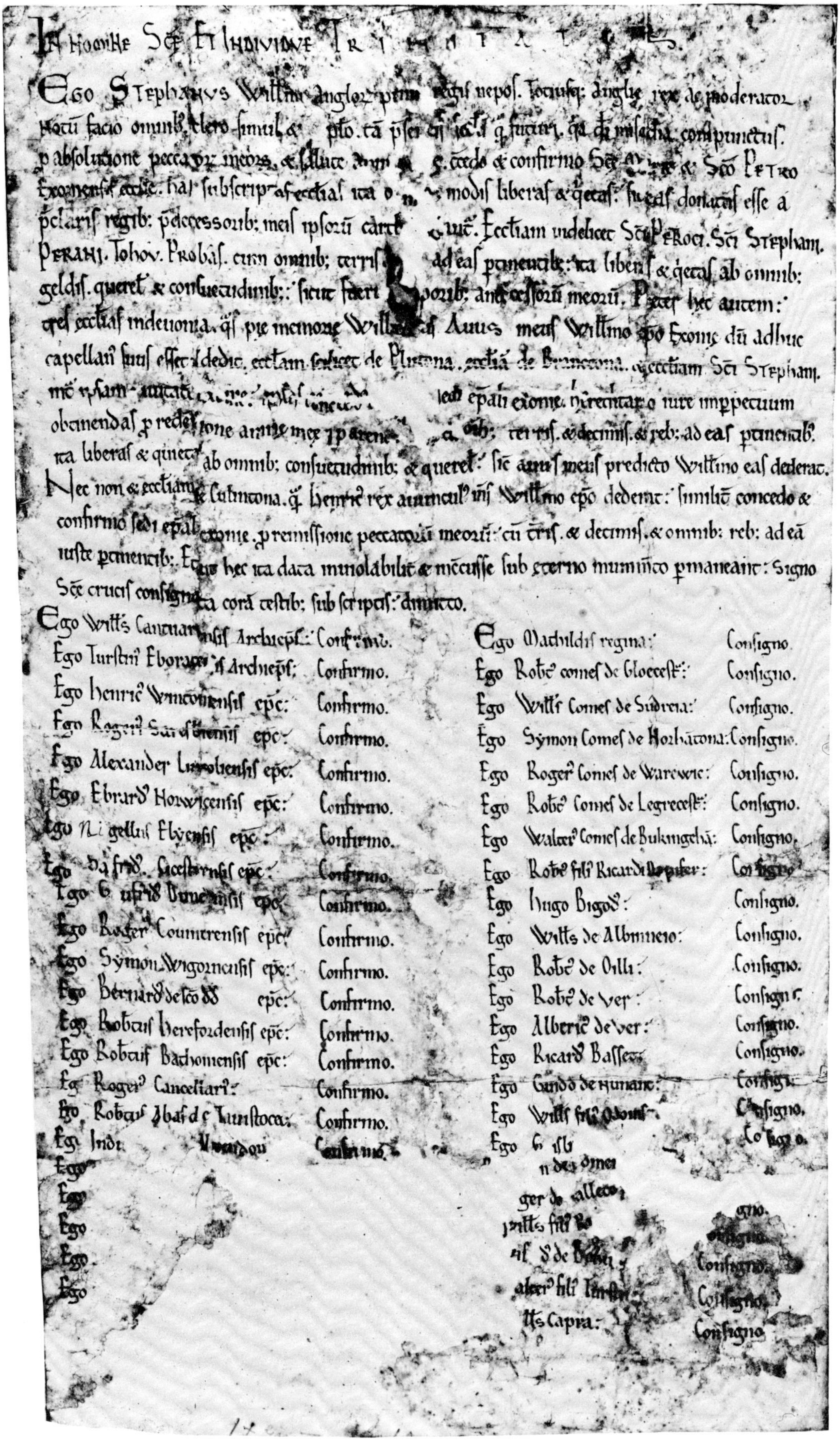
In nomine Sce et indiuidue Trinitatis.

Ego Stephanus Willelmi anglorum primi regis nepos. totiusque anglie rex de moderatore notum facio omnibus clero simul et populo. tam presentibus quam his qui futuri. quam diu misericordia consupernetis. pro absolutione peccatorum meorum. et salute [illegible] concedo et confirmo Sce [illegible] et Sco Petro Exoniensis ecclesie. has subscriptas ecclesias ita [illegible] modis liberas et quietas: sicut eas donatas esse a [illegible] regibus predecessoribus meis ipsorum cartis [illegible]. Ecclesiam uidelicet Sci Petroci. Sci Stephani. [illegible] Probas. cum omnibus terris [illegible] ad eas pertinentibus. ita liberas et quietas ab omnibus geldis. querelis et consuetudinibus: sicut fuerunt [illegible] temporibus antecessorum meorum. Preter hec autem: tres ecclesias indeuonia. quas pie memorie Willelmus [illegible] auus meus Willelmo epo Exonie dum adhuc capellanus suus esset dedit. ecclesiam scilicet de Plimtona. ecclesiam de Branctona. et ecclesiam Sci Stephani. [illegible] ipsam [illegible] sedi epali exonie. in perpetuum [illegible] obtinendas pro recte [illegible] anime mee. [illegible] cum omnibus terris. et decimis. et rebus ad eas pertinentibus. ita liberas et quietas ab omnibus consuetudinibus et querelis: sicut auus meus predicto Willelmo eas dederat.

Nec non et ecclesiam de Culmtona. quam henricus rex auunculus meus Willelmo epo dederat: similiter concedo et confirmo sedi epali exonie. pro remissione peccatorum meorum: cum terris. et decimis. et omnibus rebus ad eam iuste pertinentibus. Et [illegible] hec ita data inuiolabiliter et inconcusse sub eterno munimento permaneant: Signo Sce crucis consigna[illegible] coram testibus subscriptis: [illegible].

Ego Willelmus Cantuariensis Archiepiscopus:	Confirmo.	Ego Mathildis regina:	Consigno.
Ego Turstinus Eboracensis Archiepiscopus:	Confirmo.	Ego Robertus comes de Gloecestre:	Consigno.
Ego henricus Wintoniensis epc:	Confirmo.	Ego Willelmus Comes de Sudreia:	Consigno.
Ego Rogerus Saresberiensis epc:	Confirmo.	Ego Symon Comes de Horhantona:	Consigno.
Ego Alexander Lincoliensis epc:	Confirmo.	Ego Rogerus Comes de Warewic:	Consigno.
Ego Ebrardus Norwicensis epc:	Confirmo.	Ego Robertus Comes de Legrecestre:	Consigno.
Ego Nigellus Elyensis epc:	Confirmo.	Ego Walterus Comes de Bukingeham:	Consigno.
Ego [illegible] Cicestrensis epc:	Confirmo.	Ego Robertus filius Ricardi dapifer:	Consigno.
Ego [illegible] Dunelmensis epc:	Confirmo.	Ego hugo Bigodus:	Consigno.
Ego Rogerus Couentrensis epc:	Confirmo.	Ego Willelmus de Albinneio:	Consigno.
Ego Symon Wigornensis epc:	Confirmo.	Ego Robertus de Oilli:	Consigno.
Ego Bernardus de Sco Dd epc:	Confirmo.	Ego Robertus de Ver:	Consigno.
Ego Robertus herefordensis epc:	Confirmo.	Ego Albericus de Ver:	Consigno.
Ego Robertus Bathoniensis epc:	Confirmo.	Ego Ricardus Basset:	Consigno.
Ego Rogerus Cancellarius:	Confirmo.	Ego [illegible] de Humaz:	Consigno.
Ego Robertus Abbas de Tunstoca:	Confirmo.	Ego Willelmus filius Odonis:	Consigno.
Ego [illegible]	Confirmo.	Ego [illegible]	Consigno.
Ego		[illegible]	
Ego		[illegible]ger de [illegible]	
Ego		Willelmus filius Ro[illegible]	[illegible]gno.
Ego		[illegible] de [illegible]	Consigno.
Ego		[illegible] filius [illegible]	Consigno.
Ego		[illegible] Capra:	Consigno.
		[illegible]lls Capra:	Consigno.

a (London, Muniments of the Dean and Chapter of St. Paul's, A60/36)

No. **562**

Date: 1139–54, at London.

King Stephen orders that the Bishop of London and his canons (of St. Paul's) shall hold their lands and men as freely and quit as in the time of any of his predecessors.

This writ (*precipio*) is in the hand of an unidentified scribe. There are some suspicious features. Externally, the most noticeable is the wide margin on either side, which seems normally to have been avoided by royal scribes. It is difficult to see why the writ should have been addressed to all justices, sheriffs, barons, officials, and lieges of England rather than in the fuller 'general' form. The writ bears some resemblance to **563**, which refers to the London and Middlesex lands of St. Paul's, and **564**, which refers to the Essex and Hertfordshire lands. Each of these bears the precisely specified and appropriate shire court address and each is a writ (*precipio*) with the same single witness and the same place-date as the present example. We know the other two writs only from cartulary copies and, although they cannot properly provide a standard of comparison with an original, we think their wording has an authentic ring. In the present writ (line 2) *Precipio ut episcopus Londoniensis et canonici sui teneant* etc. is not a usual phrase in royal writs. The *canonici ecclesie sancti Pauli* of the other two writs or *ecclesia sancti Pauli et canonici ibidem deo servientes* would be more usual. Similarly, the confirmatory words (lines 3–5) *sicut antecessores sui . . . sicut testantur karte W. regis et H. regis* are not completely in accordance with those commonly used by royal scribes. These diplomatic features alone would not condemn the writ as spurious and since it is endorsed in a thirteenth-century hand *carta dupplicata S. regis super libertatibus* it may have been intended only as a copy. We are, however, obliged to treat it with some suspicion.

b (Oxford, The Bodleian Library, MS. charters, Essex a. 4, No. 84)

No. **228**

Date: 1139–54, at London.

King Stephen orders Ralph de Sackville to restore to the monks of St. John's Abbey, Colchester, possession of half a hide of land in Wickham Skeith (Suffolk) and two men living there.

Written by an unidentified scribe in a 'court' hand, this is a perfectly straightforward writ (*precipio*) addressed, presumably, to the disseisor, ordering him to reseise the complainants, and it includes the clause common and appropriate to such writs, *Et nisi feceris W. de Ipra faciet ne clamorem inde audiam pro recti penuria*.

PLATE XLIII

S. Ren angl'. Justic. Vic Baron'. 7 Omnib; ministr' 7 fidelib; suis Toci[us]
anglie. sal'. P[re]cipio q[uo]d ep[iscopu]s Lond'. 7 canonic[i] sui teneant om[ne]s t[er]ras.
7 ho[m]i[n]es suos infra burga 7 ext'. libe 7 q[ui]ete in om[n]ib; sic antecessores
sui u[m]qua liberi[us]. 7 q[ui]eti[us] tenue[run]t t[em]p[or]e alicui[us] Regis. 7 sic testant[ur]
Carte W. Regis. 7 h. Regis. 7 Ric' deluci. ap[ud] Lond'.

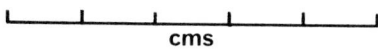

a

cms

S. Rex Angl'. ... icec Villa. sal'. P[re]cipio ...
... Monach[i] de Cole[cestr]e. ... in Wicha[m] ...
... ep[iscop]e in om[n]ib[us]. sic[ut] inde meli[us] saisiti fue[run]t ...
...

b

84

(Ely Cathedral, Archives of the Dean and Chapter, Charter 7)

No. **262**

Date: June 1139–March 1140, at Cambridge.

King Stephen confirms to the monks of Ely all their property and tenures: the penalties of royal justice will be exacted from those who take anything from the monks in defiance of this royal command.

This charter is written in the formal 'book' hand of an unidentified scribe, who was probably employed by the beneficiaries. In the superscription Stephen is given not only the royal title but that of *Dux Normannorum* which, although possible at the time when we believe this document to have been issued, was rarely used at any time during his reign, except in the legends on the equestrian sides of his seals. The address, too, is in an unusual form, including earls and barons as well as justices, sheriffs, and officials in places where the monks of Ely hold land, with the further addition of lieges (*fideles*), French and English, of all England. In the dispositive clause the words *in tempore alicuius regis uel episcopi tenuerunt cum omnibus consuetudinibus quas carte ecclesie confirmant et testificantur* (lines 5–6) stand out, since they commit the king to a wide and ill-defined guarantee of charters which there is no indication that he had seen. Royal and other professional scriptores usually avoided anything so dangerously vague. *Et precipio* (line 6), which might have been expected to introduce an ordinary injunctive clause, deals with a different matter, namely, the contingency of violent dispossession of the monks and the royal forfeiture which this would entail for offenders. In general this writ is drafted in a form which may have been legally acceptable, but which does not conform to the standards of professional scriptores whether in the royal or in other service. It looks like the work of someone who would have been much more at home in writing or copying manuscripts of a literary rather than a legal and administrative kind.

PLATE XLIV

cms

a (London, The Public Record Office, E. 40/15394)

No. **446**

Date: 1139–47, at London.

King Stephen confirms to Lewes Priory the gifts of William, Earl of Warenne, in lands, churches, tithes, and all property.

This charter of confirmation is written in a clear 'book' hand by an unidentified scribe, who was probably employed by Lewes Priory. *β* and *ꝗ* ligatures are used but there are no signs of cursive writing. In contrast to the charters issued for Lewes by identified royal Scriptores (Pls. XX *b*, XXXIV *b*, XXXV *a–b*), the seal was not on a tongue but (supposedly) on a tag passed through two slits in the fold. As regards its drafting, it might be called a writ-charter in the classical form of a confirmation in the manner of the royal Scriptorium. The superscription and 'general' address are impeccably correct and the dispositive and injunctive clauses contain all that is necessary, without any waste of words. Clearly, it was the earl, as donor, who would first have been pledged to warranty in case of need. This royal confirmation would have provided a valuable, indeed a necessary, safeguard.

b (London, The Public Record Office, E. 40/14890)

No. **516**

Date: 1135–54, at Westminster.

King Stephen has granted the land of Clayhurst, in Beckenham (Kent) to the Priory of Holy Trinity, Aldgate, for a rent of 12*d*. per annum.

This is written by an unidentified scribe who was very economical in his use of parchment. It is addressed to R. Malismanis, who may have been the reeve, and the men of Beckenham. It is in the briefest possible terms. The single witness, Hubert the Chamberlain, was the chamberlain of the Queen. This is an interesting fact since the Queen, as lady of the honour of Boulogne, was patron of Holy Trinity, Aldgate. It may well be that she had this writ written by one of her own scribes and merely presented it to her husband for authentication with his seal. It may date from the period before her son Eustace was created Count.

PLATE XLV

a

cms

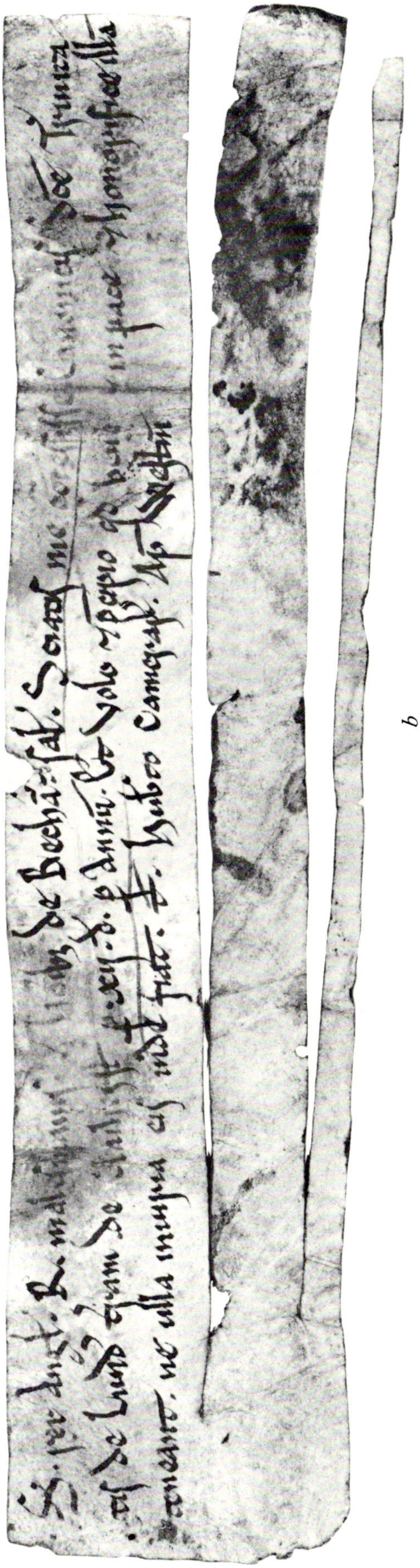

b

(London, The British Museum, Additional Charter 19579)

No. **703**

Date: Ostensibly 1144–7, and perhaps 1144, at Devizes.

The Empress Maud grants Blewbury (Berks.) to Reading Abbey.
  The scribe has not been identified. This is one of a pair of pretended originals, the other being
B.M. Add. Ch. 19577 of which a facsimile is given in Warner and Ellis, i. 22. Of the two, this one,
which has a tongue and tie but no seal, looks the more plausible. The other, with a fold and cord but
no seal, was probably copied from it with some antiquarian additions. The superscription of this
charter is correct for a date after Maud's assumption of the title *Anglorum Domina* and the
general address is also of a normal kind. The text of the charter, however, consists of a dispositive
clause, which begins with an elaborate 'movent' and continues in a form more characteristic of
an injunctive clause, though the transition is not marked by the customary *Quare volo et firmiter
precipio* or similar phrase. The witnesses are possible for a date not earlier than Christmas, 1143,
when Roger fitz Miles succeeded to the earldom of Hereford or later than 31 Oct. 1147, when
Robert Earl of Gloucester, died.

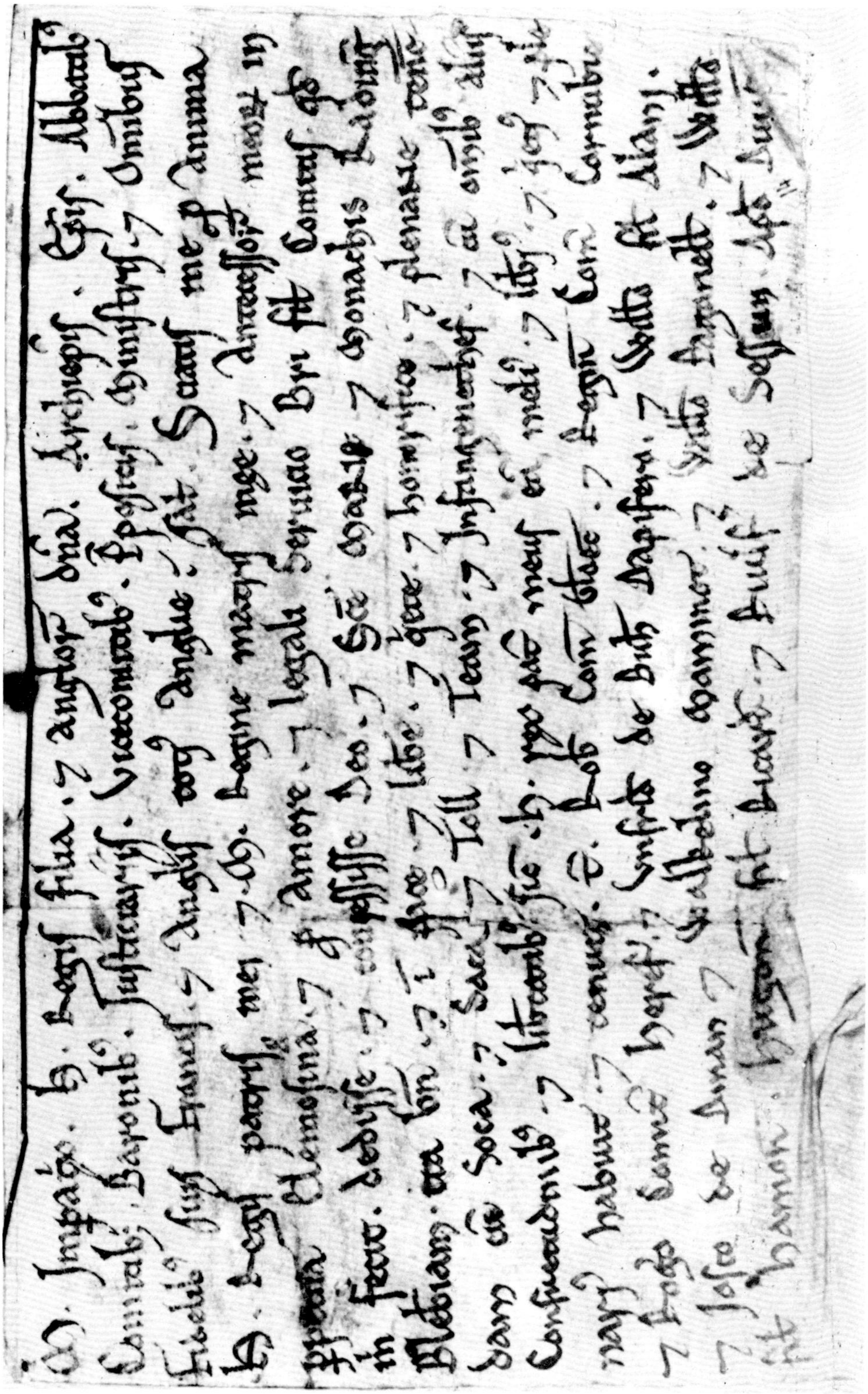

PLATE XLVI

M . Inpatꝯ . h . Regis filia . 7 anglor̄ dña . Archiepꝰ . Epis . Abbatiꝰ
Comitiꝰ Baroniꝰ . Justiciariꝰ . Vicecomitabꝰ . Ppositꝭ . Ministriꝰ 7 Omnibus
fidelib suis Francis . 7 Anglis corꝰ Anglie : ſalt . Sciatis me p̄ anima
h . Regis patris mei . 7 Or . Regine matris mee . 7 Antecessorꝰ meoꝝ . 7
ꝑpetuam elemoſinā . 7 p̄ amore . 7 legali servicio Bꝰr̄ . At Comitis . co
in feuo . dedisse . 7 conceſſiſſe Deo . 7 Sc̄e Marie . 7 Monachis . . . .
Eccliam . ex bn̄ . 7 i. . . . 7 ꝗea . 7 gꝛe . 7 honorifice . 7 plenarie tenē
sam c̄ō Soca . 7 Saca . 7 Toll . 7 Team . 7 Infangenethef . 7 ex om̄ib aliꝗ
Consuetudiniꝰ . 7 libtatiꝰ fic jp̄ qd meꝰ et mei . 7 ttꝯ . 7 qꝺ tꝭ ꝗle
ꝛayꝯ habuiꝰ tenuit . 7 tenuiꝰ . De . Loꝯ Comiti Chr̄e . 7 Regni Com Cornubie
7 Hugo Somt̄ Iꝰꝺ . 7 cōfirð se Butꝭ dapifem . 7 Wltē ft Alani .
7 Joſce de Amar . 7 Walterno Camerar . Wltē Pignell . 7 Wltē
ſ amor̄g. fr . Ricarꝺ . Apud Sar̄ . . . .

(London, The British Museum, Add. Charter 75724)

No. **116**

Date: 25 July 1141–24 June 1142, at Devizes.

The Empress 'founds' Bordesley Abbey and confirms its possessions.

This handsome charter was found in an oval box of very thin wood, with a description on the lid in an eighteenth-century hand, together with a bag of silver pennies, behind a secret panel in an old cabinet belonging to the Willes family. It had belonged to Clement Throckmorton of Haseley, Warwickshire, c. 1640 and by 1871–2 had come into the possession of William Willes of Goodrest, Reading [*Sir Christopher Hatton's Book of Seals* ed. L. C. Loyd and D. M. Stenton, 1950, No. 514 and H. M. C. Second and Third Reports]. Thence it went to the Willes family house at Newbold Comyn, Warwickshire and so to Edward Willes Esq. of Honnington, Shipston-on-Stour, who sold it to the British Museum in July, 1968. It is excellently preserved and the parchment and the ink look as fresh as on the day it was written. The seal, attached to the bottom fold by a long tag of white kid- or doe-skin, is also in very good condition, since it is protected by a bag of heavy woven silk, with a pattern of crosses in bright blue and gold, the colours showing no sign of fading.

The firm, formal handwriting is very similar to, probably identical with, that of **115**, also in favour of Bordesley Abbey, which includes all the witnesses of the present charter and three others and bears the same place-date. The charter in which the Empress confirmed to Osney Abbey the church of St. George in Oxford Castle, **632**, is also written in a hand which resembles this. Handsome though the charter reproduced here is in externals, the draftsmanship is not that of a scribe well versed in English ways. The dispositive clause opens (line 2) with the words *Notum sit vobis* instead of the almost invariable *Sciatis* of royal charters. There is a slip of the pen where the scribe has written *cum totam terram* (line 4) and another where he has written *in bene* (line 8). There is no injunctive clause in proper form but, instead, a garbled clause which combines a reaffirmation of the confirmation, together with a clause of authentication appropriate to a final protocol such as Scriptor XIII not infrequently used (line 8): *Hec autem omnia libere et quiete in* (sic) *bene et in pace ab omni servitio et exactione et consuetudine seculari imperpetuum permansura concedo et sigilli mei impressione confirmo.* This betrays confusion in the mind of the scribe as to how the charter ought properly to proceed at this important point. The composition of **115** shows similar uncertainty, but the scribe of **632** was able to draft a charter in acceptable English regal form.

It should be added that the original founder of the abbey was Waleran Count of Meulan in 1138. At that time he was supporting King Stephen. When he went over to the Empress in the second half of 1141, he apparently purchased her favour by making her the 'founder' of this abbey. Subsequently she also took over his foundation of Le Valasse in Normandy (see G. H. White in *T.R.H.S.*, 4th series, xvii (1934) 32, 40–1). The 'foundation' of a religious house had many stages—the grant of a site, the arrival of the religious, and the erection of permanent buildings. See V. H. Galbraith in *Cambridge Historical Journal*, iv (1934), 205–22 and 296–8.

PLATE XLVII

M. Impatrix H. reg filia 7 Anglor dña. Archiepis. Epis. Abbib. Comitib. Baron. Iustic. Vicecomitib; 7 oïmb; fidelib; Angl 7 Norm. Tam pñtenab; quam futuris. fal. Notum sit nob; me p dei amore 7 p aïa H reg patris mei. 7 M. regine matris mee. 7 antecessor meoz. 7 p salute G. com Andeg 7 dñi mei. 7 h. heredis mei 7 alioz filioz meoz. 7 p pace 7 stabilitate regni Angl. fundasse abbiam qñdam q dr Bordeslea. de ordine Cisterciens. in honore beatissime virginis Marie 7 gñne Celor. Huic auc abbie dedi 7 concessi 7 confirmaui Totã terrã Bordeslee. 7 Tuneshale. 7 Ludeshale. 7 Cobeslae. 7 bolessurie. pt terrã parcaq; 7 totã dñicariu Budsforde. 7 Hozbune. in bosco 7 plano. in prateis 7 pasturis. in aquis 7 molendinis. 7 in omnib; aliis pauenacis. Ptea ius aduocationis 7 donationis eccłie de Tydeburga cum virgata terre. in eade villa. 7 quicq'd facias. ppe dñisa terre eclē abbie. 7 nouü puteü de Wich de ppo labore suo. 7 omnia dispatica sua. in foresta de freccham. cu omni ldoaire pannagq; 7 pasture. 7 mareperiu ad edificia construenda. 7 altaria seru usuq; necessariaru. 7 una piscatiã apd herncleiã. cu tra q ad eã ptinec. Hec auc omia libr 7 quiete in bene 7 in pace ab omni seruicio 7 exactione 7 consuetudine seculari nup'tui pmansura. concedo 7 sigilli mei nup'sione confirmo. Test Rot. com Gloecestr. 7 Gualgram com mett. 7 Milon com hereford. 7 Wuhlo de Belloc. 7 Brito d'ssablaco. 7 Gaufrid de Walcnut. 7 Goscelmo de Ballol. 7 Rob de frumouatt. .... com hereford. 7 Wuhlo de ponz arch Camer. apd dnis.

cms

(Salisbury Cathedral, Muniments of the Dean and Chapter, C.2)

No. **787**

Date: 25 Dec. 1139, at Salisbury.

King Stephen quitclaims the prebendal lands of St. Mary's, Salisbury, in whatsoever shires they are, of Danegeld and confirms to the canons the churches which Bishop Roger had acquired and given them.

This charter is written by the same scribe **c** who wrote **313** (Pl. L) and **788** (Pl. XLIX). It resembles the kind of hand used by royal scribes. This charter and **788** bear the same date and have in common all the witnesses in this one. The words *regia auctoritate corroboro* (line 4) should be noted, for they represent a less elaborate form of a clause frequently used by Scriptor XIII and occasionally by some other scribes. They have an ecclesiastical ring. There is no single phrase in this charter which could not have been used in the royal Scriptorium and the general diplomatic structure would not excite suspicion. It is far otherwise with the augmented version (**788**) which will be found in the next plate.

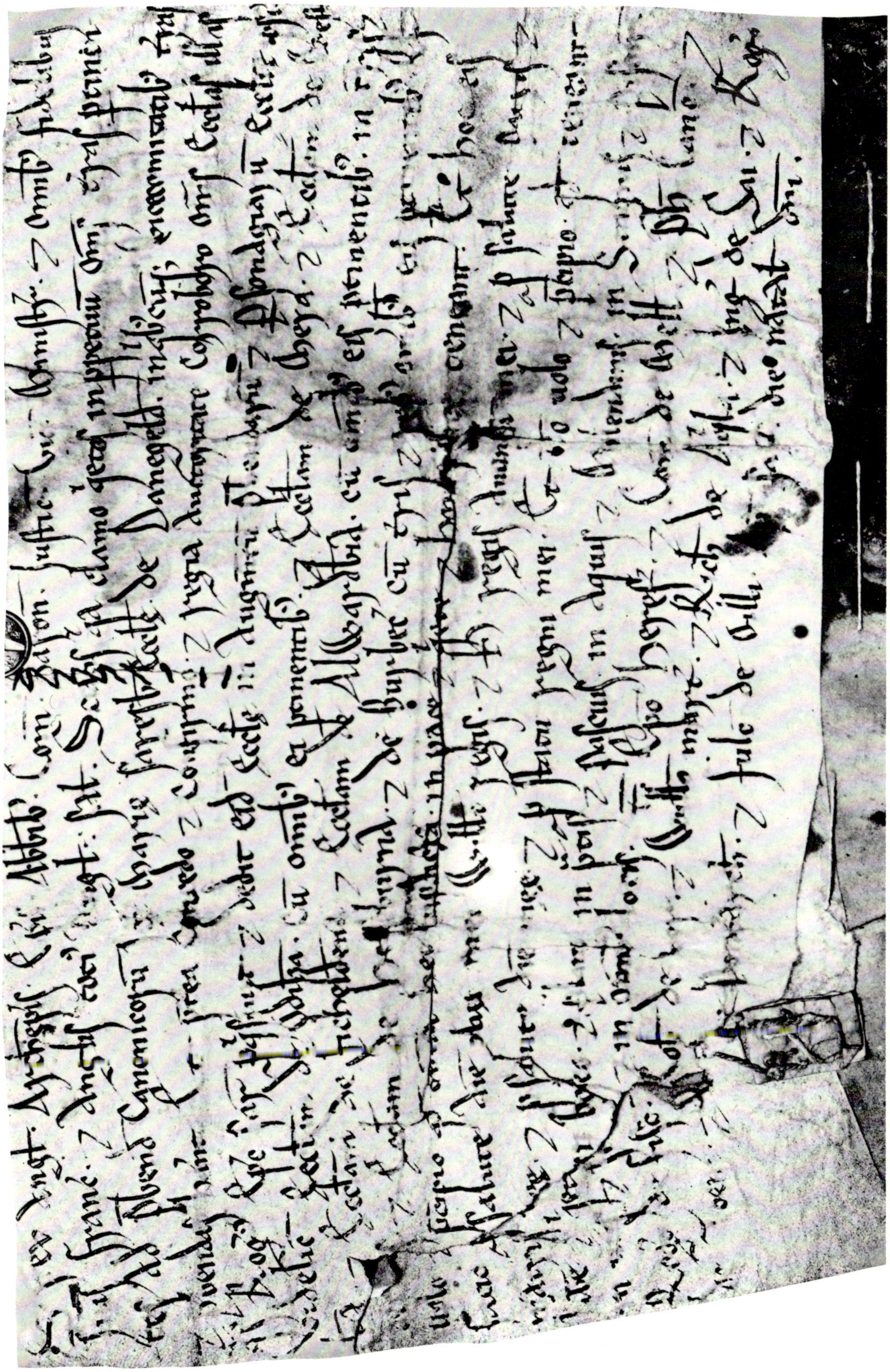

PLATE XLVIII

(Salisbury Cathedral, Muniments of the Dean and Chapter, C.2)

No. **788**

Date: 25 Dec. 1139, at Salisbury.

King Stephen quitclaims the prebendal lands of the canons of St. Mary's, Salisbury, of Danegeld and confirms the churches which Bishop Roger had acquired and given to the canons and, in addition, gives them ten librates of royal demesne.

This charter is written in the hand of the scribe who wrote that shown in the previous plate. It bears the same date, namely Christmas Day (1139) but there are several additional witnesses, those who follow William de Pont de l'Arche, with the exception of Fulk d'Oilly. The space in line 7, left for the insertion of the name of the place where the ten librates of royal demesne were situated, would not normally have been allowed in a document issued from the royal Scriptorium nor, in all probability, in one scrutinized and officially authenticated by the royal seal. In the injunctive clause (line 9) where the traditional formula *in bosco et plano* etc. is used, the words *extra castellum et infra* are unusual, and this together with the additional grants, from *Et nominatim ecclesiam* (line 5) up to the blank space (line 7) at the end of the dispositive clause, seems suspiciously closely related to the agreement of 9 April 1152 (**796**) whereby Duke Henry was to hold Devizes Castle for three years. Such a document might be a conflation and must be held suspect.

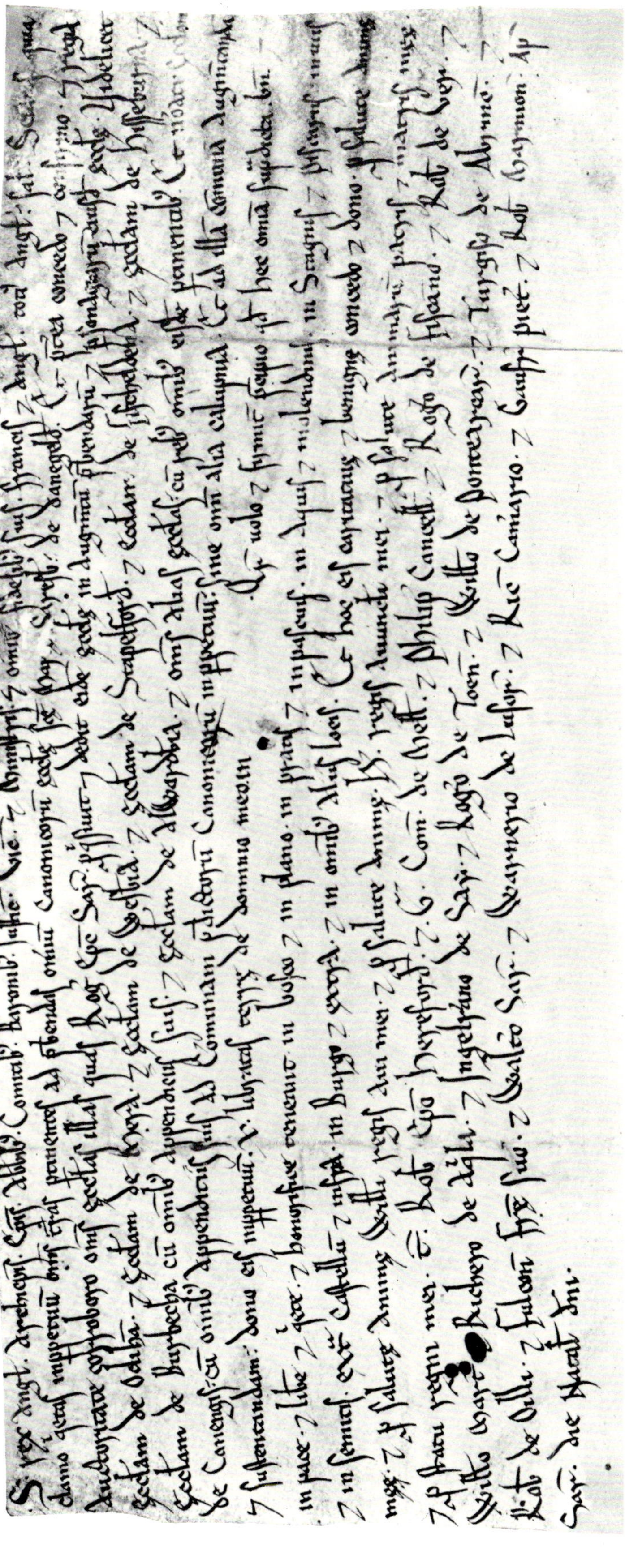

PLATE XLIX

(London, The Public Record Office, D.L. 25/2)

No. **313**

Date: *c.* 1138, at Malmesbury.

This writ (*precipio*), issued by Roger, Bishop of Salisbury, in his capacity of Chief Justiciar (though this is not specifically stated) orders Sibilla, widow of Payn fitz John, immediately to reseise Roger fitz Miles, her son-in-law, of all the lands *de accatis* of her late husband, with the corn etc., which he gave to Roger on his marriage with his eldest daughter Cecilia (see **312** and Pl. XXI).

In external appearance this writ exactly resembles a royal writ, though the tongue for the seal is very narrow, hardly broader than the wrapper. It is in the hand of scribe **c** who wrote **787** (Plate XLVIII) and **788** (Plate XLIX—a suspect document) and who may have been the chaplain or secretary of Bishop Roger.[1] The writ consists of an injunctive clause only and its interest lies in the fact that it is issued by the Bishop *ex parte regis et mea* (lines 1–2), which indicates that he must have been acting as Chief Justiciar.

This is a rare survival from Stephen's reign. The king spent very little time abroad. His only recorded visit to the Continent was to Normandy in 1137. There can have been little occasion for viceregal writs or justiciarial writs, such as this, after the fall of Bishop Roger and his relatives in June 1139, though it is to be noted that the queen acted (and very vigorously, too) on her husband's behalf during his imprisonment. In our opinion this writ is subsequent to **312**, which can be dated December 1137, and cannot have been issued as a viceregal writ during Stephen's absence in Normandy. It must belong to the period between December 1137 and June 1139.

A distinction is drawn between the lands (with their produce) which Payn fitz John acquired *de accatis* and those which he had inherited. His widow seems to have argued that the lands acquired (*de accatis*), or their produce should rightfully pass to her and not go with the inherited lands to Payn's daughter and her husband. It appears from this writ that the legal decision at the highest level went against her.

[1] T. A. M. Bishop, *Scriptores Regis*, 28.

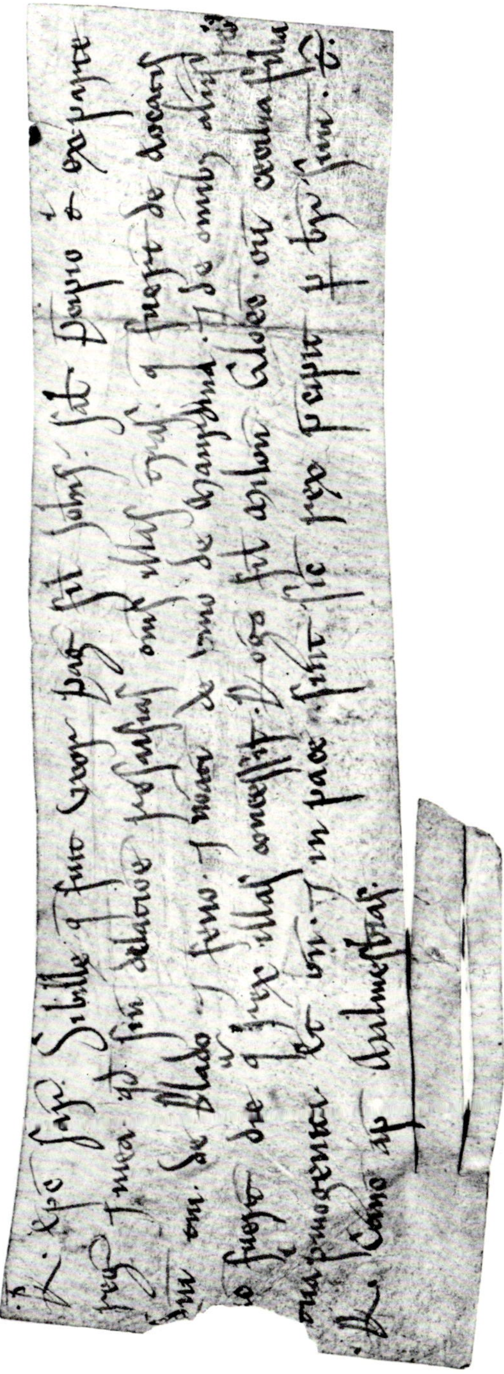